TECH PREP EDUCATION

Tech Prep Education
A Total Quality Approach

CHARLES J. LAW, JR., Ed.D.
EDUCATIONAL CONSULTANT

TECHNOMIC
PUBLISHING CO., INC.
LANCASTER · BASEL

Tech Prep Education
a **TECHNOMIC**® publication

Published in the Western Hemisphere by
Technomic Publishing Company, Inc.
851 New Holland Avenue, Box 3535
Lancaster, Pennsylvania 17604 U.S.A.

Distributed in the Rest of the World by
Technomic Publishing AG
Missionsstrasse 44
CH-4055 Basel, Switzerland

Printed in the United States of America
10 9 8 7 6 5 4 3 2

Main entry under title:
  Tech Prep Education: A Total Quality Approach

A Technomic Publishing Company book
Bibliography: p. 231
Includes index p. 237

Library of Congress Catalog Card No. 93-60982
ISBN No. 1-56676-086-0

*To Gerald B. James, whose actions have always exemplified
what he taught, and who has spent his life
opening doors through which many of us have walked.*

CONTENTS

FOREWORD

AMERICAN education in many ways is still based on the traditional, book-centered curriculum of the industrial age. Because of advances in technology and in our knowledge of how children learn, there is clearly a need for fundamental change, if we are to prepare America's youth for higher education and the workplace. In a world in which skills overshadow content, we must provide experiences that will encourage students to solve problems, to become adept at using technology, to think, to use research as a vehicle to learn, and to base their learning on conceptual and technical knowledge.

Innovations are flooding our schools; many of them will be successful because they will be created, implemented and evaluated by those who best understand what education should be about—the teachers and the students. One of the most exciting initiatives in this country is Tech Prep, a movement that is challenging the education scene with energy and promise. Until now, there have been few resources to which educators could turn to understand the conceptual framework of Tech Prep and its connection to other reform initiatives. In this book, Charles Law provides that framework and puts an unerring finger on the problems facing local superintendents and their faculties as they plan the incorporation of Tech Prep into comprehensive school reform.

More importantly, Dr. Law has developed a process for answering today's questions and for discerning problems that may emerge in the future. By doing so, he has created a guide for education reform that transcends Tech Prep. I commend this book to all educators and, most particularly, to district and school administrators who may be considering or involved in school reform and in the formation of a holistic curriculum.

Werner Rogers, Ed.D.
State Superintendent of Schools
Georgia Department of Education

PREFACE

THIS book devotes a lion's share of its attention to the complex and often misunderstood relationship that exists between tech prep, the subject of this work, and vocational education. This should not suggest that the two are synonymous; they are not. Yet, if tech prep is to succeed (which requires releasing the enormous energy and potential of instruction rooted in the reality of the work world), it must embody the pedagogy and educational philosophy of the most effective practices of vocational education. This seeming paradox requires unpacking the ofttimes latent instructional energy of vocational education from its traditional packages and repackaging it to meet the needs of students of today and tomorrow.

The author, however, has no fear that tech prep will bring about the demise of vocational education. Whether or not the curriculum and instructional packages labeled so precisely over the past seventy-five years (i.e., academic education, college prep, general education, and vocational education) survive is not the point. Nor is the survival of tech prep itself important in the long term.

The point is that American society is beginning to see all work as a part of the life of every person. We are tearing down the old dualism that holds *thinking work* to be more important and prestigious than *doing work*. And because education always reflects its societal context, it appears to be reversing its historically ineffective book-centered approach, replacing it with instructional strategies that are applied, context-specific, experiential, rooted in reality, and connected with the evolving world of work. Both vocational education and tech prep have much to offer that reformation process.

It is time for educators and others to recognize that this realistic and more effective approach to teaching and learning is of increasing importance, and to eliminate any vestiges of narrow-mindedness surrounding such topics as which educational strategies belong to whom, specific groups of students being able to understand concepts and theories better than others, and certain types of education being more ''acceptable.'' It is time, instead, to recognize that the job of educating America's youth is big enough to share and to pool the available resources for the good of everyone involved, especially the students. Tech prep offers just that kind of opportunity.

ACKNOWLEDGEMENTS

THE contributions of the following persons to the writing of this book are gratefully acknowledged, and I wish to express my sincerest gratitude to:

Camilla, my wife and my best friend, in whose love and devotion I find new depths and exciting surprises every day.

Amy, Jamie, and Jerel, our children, whose faith in me often exceeded my own and carried me through many difficult times.

My parents, who very early taught me the value of dedication, hard work, and prayer.

Cayce C. Scarborough, a "master teacher," who showed me the connection between philosophical thinking and effective teaching.

Rupert Evans, Gordon Swanson, Peirce Hammond, Denny Wolfe, Cliff Belcher, and Jim Lunsford, friends and scholars all, who spent untold hours reading early drafts and offering positive and insightful criticism of the manuscript.

Mel Miller, who has continued an almost single-handed quest for the philosophic roots of vocational education.

My many good friends in vocational education; especially Dan Dunham, Carl Lamar (deceased), Bob Mullen, Katy Greenwood, Don Brannon, Gil Woolard, Monte Multannen, Darrell Parks, Roy Irons, Francis Tuttle, Trudy Anderson, Frank Santoro, Anne Matthews, Barbara James (deceased), Carrol Burchinal, Marge Harouff, Billy Johnson, Neils Brooks, Ned Swartz, and Madeleine Hemmings, all of whom have influenced my thinking.

My friends in the larger sphere of education; Bob Hill, Craig Phillips, Werner Rogers, Reeves McGlohon, Wayne Teague, Charlie Williams, Dan Pilkinton, Harold Fisher, Laura Mast, Dorothy Zimmerman, John Hopkins, Preston Kronkosky, and Dena Stoner, each of whom has contributed in important ways.

Joseph L. Eckenrode and Susan G. Farmer of Technomic Publishing Company, who held my hand and led me through the intricacies of turning my early thoughts into a publishable document.

And, most of all, Almighty God, Whose Grace truly is sufficient.

INTRODUCTION

TECH prep has taken the country by storm. The concept was first introduced in the mid-1980s by Dale Parnell as a response to the plight of those students to whom he gave the name, the *Neglected Majority*, and the term itself came into popular usage shortly thereafter (Hull, 1991). Since then, interest in tech prep and its subsequent growth have been phenomenal, and local tech prep initiatives continue to spring up at a prodigious rate, with no apparent end in sight.

The author's concern about this rush to implement tech prep was the genesis of this book. In far too many instances, tech prep is being grasped with all the fervor of a drowning person reaching for a life preserver and, in truth, with no more critical review than one would give such a life-saving device, if one were really going under. The irony of the situation is that, while the concept of tech prep may embody much of what education needs at this time, unless those who use it understand its true potential for effecting long-term educational and organizational change and incorporate it into their comprehensive plans for reform, they may settle for its utility in keeping their heads above water in the immediate emergency, then discard it in favor of another tactic the next time disaster strikes.

For example, in many places, tech prep is viewed simply as an up-dated and slightly revised program of vocational education. In other cases, it is implemented as a third curriculum track, comprised of a series of applied academic courses, which have no connection to either vocational or college preparatory education. Although a comprehensive vision of tech prep incorporates the very best of traditional vocational education *and* academic education, it embodies a much larger concept than either one of these alone. At its best, tech prep is a comprehensive educational reform *strategy* based in curriculum and instruction. Seen from this perspective, it can contribute to major educational change and reform.

To make use of tech prep in this fashion and connect it with the other major educational reform initiatives (e.g., total quality education, outcome-based education, or cooperative learning) requires a conceptual understanding. This book builds such a conceptual foundation, beginning with the major contextual factors that are shaping tech prep and ending with a clear statement of pedagogy and educational philosophy. The reader is encouraged to work through the entire process of building the conceptual foundation and thus own not only the information presented in this book, but, more importantly, the process itself.

Tech Prep: An Educational Reform Strategy

TOTAL quality education (TQE), cooperative learning, outcome-based education (OBE), site-based management, and technical preparatory education (tech prep): these are among the hottest topics on today's educational reform agenda. Collectively, they affect millions of American students. Tech prep alone enrolled nearly a half million students during 1992 (Organizational Affiliates, 1992). Yet, with one exception, the proponents of these initiatives do not seem to recognize the need to make connections between and among them.

That exception, total quality education (TQE), focuses on improving educational systems, rather than courses or programs, by applying the concepts of total quality management (TQM). Total quality management is itself a systematic process through which an organization's managers and employees use Deming's Fourteen Points or principles of transformation to translate their core mission into one of consistently meeting the expectations of their consumers (Deming, 1986). The success of this holistic approach to improving quality is contingent upon *all* the individuals in an organization understanding the need for systemic change, their commitment *to* change, and their continuous and concerted action to make that commitment a reality (Lunsford, 1993).

TQE, therefore, requires those who implement it to connect the various components of their system (school, school district, or postsecondary institution), including its personnel (from custodian to chief administrative officer), into a holistic unit committed to improving educational quality. These kinds of connections can make all educational reform initiatives, including tech prep, more effective than any one could ever be alone.

Tech prep is particularly susceptible to the malady described above. To remedy that situation, this book:

1

1) Identifies the current strengths and weaknesses of tech prep
2) Explores the relationship between tech prep and vocational education, and identifies the contributions vocational education can make
   to tech prep and *vice versa*
3) Builds a conceptual foundation upon which practitioners can construct their own, more effective, tech prep initiatives
4) Identifies the consistencies that exist between tech prep, TQM, and
   TQE
5) Connects tech prep with TQE, and shows how the two can assist
   the school, school district, and postsecondary institution to make
   long-term systemic change and continuously improve the quality
   of the product and service provided its consumers

WHAT EXACTLY IS TECH PREP?

Tech prep is an educational restructuring strategy, centered in curriculum and instruction. Called ". . . one of the most significant innovations in the education reform movement, [it can provide] . . . a new and
vital source of energy in the revitalization of vocational technical
education" (Warnat, 1992, 1). The comprehensive vision of tech prep
proposed in this book can do more than that; indeed, it can help revitalize
all of education.

Tech prep operates through "a sequence of study beginning in high
school and continuing through at least two years of postsecondary
occupational education" (Organizational Affiliates, 1992, 1–2). Its
core is a clearly defined four- or six-year curricular pathway upon which
students move from the ninth (or eleventh) grade through two years of
technical education beyond the high school, receive an associate degree,
and enter productive employment. The movement of students along this
pathway is natural and uninterrupted, because their secondary and
postsecondary instruction is connected ("articulated") to eliminate un-
necessary gaps and artificial duplication. And most importantly, the
entire sequence is tied securely to the evolving workplace.

At the secondary level, this curricular pathway is as academically
rigorous as, and is implemented parallel to, the local school's college
preparatory (academic) offerings. However, tech prep is built upon the
competencies needed for employment in a specific sector of the emerging labor market, rather than upon arbitrary and, at times, somewhat

artificial university requirements. Its theoretical and technical content is integrated into a single program of study. Secondary and postsecondary curricula segments are articulated through both formal and informal means (e.g., articulation agreements and continuous faculty interaction). Regular consultation with representative employers ensures that the instructional content is appropriate and at a level promising student competence and employability.

Most tech prep students currently complete their instruction at cooperating technical or community colleges. However, the use of apprenticeships, both within and following the high school experience, is likely to increase as America looks for new ways to prepare a world-class workforce. Regardless of the specific configuration of the secondary and postsecondary tech prep experience, the concepts presented in this book apply.

Much of tech prep's recent growth has been spurred by funds made available through the Carl D. Perkins Vocational Education and Applied Technology Act of 1990. However, state, local, and foundation funding is multiplying the investment in many areas. And as important as the Federal funds are, it is likely that in their absence, some local innovators, realizing the need for more realistic instruction for their students, would still be experimenting with tech prep-like approaches.

However, the term "*tech prep*" is by no means definitive. Nor is tech prep a panacea, as the apparent rush to it implies. In fact, it is this almost headlong rush that calls for caution and clear thinking by educational decision makers. An overly ambitious, poorly conceived, and hasty start in tech prep or any other educational reform activity can be inappropriate, costly, and frustrating. This is one of the first lessons of total quality management (Deming, 1986). Too often, however, those who implement tech prep tend to short-circuit the planning step, wanting to get into motion, be active, look busy, and do something. Not only can limited funds be misspent through such precipitous actions, but more importantly, the power of this educational improvement strategy may be squandered, weakened, and even lost.

The lack of a consistent definition of tech prep, apart from its parent legislation, is exacerbated by even less clarity about its conceptual foundation. Practitioners need this foundation to support them as they design strategies, connect tech prep to other educational reform efforts, and evaluate its effectiveness in improving instruction for their students.

THE STATUS OF AMERICAN EDUCATION—PERCEPTION VERSUS REALITY

Tech prep, like the other educational reform front-runners mentioned above, is a response to nearly two decades of the harshest criticism experienced by public education in the past seventy-five years. This criticism has resulted in "knee-jerk" reactions by some educators, caused others to do a lot of serious "soul-searching," brought schools into confrontation with many of their constituents, and spawned the multitude of separate and distinct approaches that now comprise the educational reform agenda.

To comprehend the initiatives that confront education and specifically, the place of tech prep in this tidal wave of reform, it is important to understand the context from which they spring. This, in and of itself, is not a simple task. Part of the difficulty is discerning between the educational problems that actually exist and the *perceptions* of those problems held by many who have a vested interest in improving education. Regrettably, it is some of the perceptions, rather than the reality, that have gained the most notoriety over the past ten years.

Perception: "The Sky Is Falling"

In 1983, rank and file citizens were rudely awakened by the release of *A Nation at Risk* (National Commission on Excellence in Education, 1983). Although many of its findings came as no surprise to the educational community, this landmark document shook the very foundations of American society. Written in language that "persons on the street" could understand and marketed with a flair reminiscent of Madison Avenue, this report made clear that it was not going to be ignored. In fact, many who subscribed to the prevailing political ideology of that decade used its findings to sweep this country to a new high in educational hysteria, from which it has yet to recover completely.

A succession of high-profile studies seemed to confirm the report's findings, and at times, educators felt as if the roof were caving in around their heads. Critics seemed ready to abandon public education as the keystone to American democracy. And few of the formal leaders of American education seemed willing or able to deal with the criticisms, whether they were based in fact or not. One chief state school officer, after observing the then-Secretary of Education join the critics and add to the clamor, disappointedly characterized his action as that of a general who, after witnessing the battle from a far-off mountaintop, rides among his own troops, "shooting the walking wounded."

Reality: Problems? Yes. Disaster? Hardly.

But were the critics suggesting that American public education become a thing of the past? For the most part, the answer is a definite "no," as a careful reading of the reports themselves shows. For example, the Northeast Regional Exchange (NEREX) reviewed the major studies of that period and identified five underlying beliefs (precepts) that appeared as consistent threads in all of them. These precepts bore witness to the certainty that, at that time, Americans still believed (NEREX, 1985, 56):

1) Quality education [is] a lifelong process [and] is a universal right [of all citizens].
2) Public schools [should] continue as a mainstay of our society.
3) Quality teachers and teaching underlie improved learning.
4) Education is correlated with economic and social development.
5) [However,] accountability and leadership by all must increase.

No, Americans were by no means ready to turn their backs on public education. But the criticisms made it clear that real problems did exist and that these problems demanded the full and collective attention of the nation.

Systemic Dysfunction for Some but Not for All

While many critics fired indiscriminately at any educational feature that dared to raise its head above ground level, others (e.g., Parnell, 1985) argued that the entire system was not at fault. In fact, they said that those who were planning to attend a four-year college or university were being provided for quite nicely. Unfortunately, only about 25 percent of America's high school students were enrolled in that rigorous option.

On the other hand, the *system* (a focal point of the TQM process) was decidedly dysfunctional for a large number of students, offering them little or no direction or assistance when they needed it most. This group—approaching (and, in some cases, surpassing) 50 percent in many schools—found themselves drifting through the general curriculum, disinterested in or uninspired by locally available but traditional secondary vocational education programs. As a result, many lost interest in school and took the least demanding courses just to meet minimum graduation requirements. Others dropped out to enter what has become a permanent underclass of society (Parnell, 1985).

The results have been individually tragic and nationally catastrophic. For in addition to the personal losses experienced by each of these students, it is also upon these same students, by virtue of their sheer number if for no other reason, that the rest of Americans must place their greatest hope for remaining competitive in the international labor market and maintaining their relatively high standard of living (Hodgkinson, 1985).

EDUCATION AND THE POLITICAL AGENDA

As the 1990s began and the economy refused to budge from a serious slump that had begun several years earlier, some critics suggested that American schools bore a major portion of the responsibility:

> The schools are failing their core academic mission, particularly in the more rigorous areas of study—math, science, foreign languages—so critical to a future of sophisticated technology and international competition. (Chubb and Moe, 1990, 1)

Not surprisingly, therefore, the plight of education and what to do about it became caught up in the politics of the times. A good example is *America 2000*, the Bush Administration's strategy to "reinvent" America's schools. At an historic education summit, the president and the governors of most of the states agreed upon national education goals and attempted to set the nation on a pathway to meet those goals (National Education Goals Panel, 1991). While this kind of concern may be commendable, the political arena demands quick solutions, whereas systemic educational problems do not give way to easy answers. Oftentimes, the political propensity to legislate solutions results, at best, in little or no improvement and at worst, in creating even more serious problems.

Educational practitioners need to understand both the positive and negative aspects of mixing political and educational agenda. For example, while *America 2000* caught the fancy of many governors, other political leaders, much of the business community, and some educators, Berryman and Bailey (1992) argued that it perpetuated the deep division between education and the economic preparation of all students. The possibility of such inconsistencies between true educational reform and political expediency is the reason an understanding of corporate and political pressures is included as a prominent feature in the conceptual foundation developed on the following pages.

A DIFFERENT AND MORE HOPEFUL VIEW

On the heels of *America 2000*, however, came a more positive view. By then, according to Cetron and Gayle (1991), the quality of American education was on the way up and headed back to the excellence that had once made it the envy of the world. And Susan Chira (1992) of the New York Times News Service reported that "although most Americans probably think that schools are worse than ever, the defenders of U.S. schools argue that they are as good or even better than before." For example, according to Harold Hodgkinson, director of the Center for Demographic Policy at the Institute for Educational Leadership: "The top 15 percent of America's students are world class on any set of indicators" (Hodgkinson, 1992, 8).

Others have not only questioned the prophets of doom but have challenged the basis of their claims. For example, David Berliner (1992) wrote a scathing analysis of current "politically correct" criticisms of education, specifically *America 2000*, whose goals, he claimed, did not even come close to addressing the real problems of students and schools. Finally, Berryman and Bailey presented one of the most important and illuminating points yet made in this national debate:

> . . . our concerns [about education were not] prompted by *A Nation at Risk* and similar reports. . . . [which] associated the U.S. economic decline with the deterioration in the quality of education, identifying higher standards and stiffer academic requirements (the "new basics") as the solution. We sensed that these reports had seriously misdiagnosed the problem and that the new basics would not solve it.
>
> . . . [Instead], a powerful research base, cognitive science,[1] revealed that schooling, especially its pedagogy, was poorly organized for learning, whatever the economic environment in which individuals had to deploy

---

[1]Cognitive science is an interdisciplinary field that ". . . encompasses psychologists, linguists, anthropologists, computer scientists, philosophers, and neuroscientists. The word 'cognitive' refers to perceiving and knowing, and cognitive science is the science of the mind. Cognitive scientists seek to understand perceiving, thinking, remembering, understanding language, learning, and the other mental phenomena" (Berryman and Bailey, 1992, 5).

what they knew. What was startling was that the two strands came together. The skill requirements of restructured workplaces and optimal ways of organizing learning fit one another. (Berryman and Bailey, 1992, 1–2)

THE RESPONSE OF EDUCATION

The responses of educators to the criticisms are myriad and cover many more topics than will be discussed here. This book focuses on secondary schools, two-year postsecondary institutions, and apprenticeship programs in which students are prepared for entering the work force and/or higher education.

Even in this circumscribed arena, proposals abound. There are those who advocate doing away with the general curriculum at the secondary level. Others suggest that all vocational education should be moved to postsecondary institutions. Still others recommend that vocational education be maintained in the secondary schools but that its academic rigor be increased. And more and more are suggesting that an apprenticeship option be added for high school students.

On somewhat the same wave length, but with some critical differences, Berryman and Bailey (1992) propose "cognitive apprenticeships," a pedagogical approach based upon successful apprenticeship training strategies. Others say the content of secondary school subjects should be broadened to the point where the distinction between academic and vocational education subjects becomes blurred. Many are coming to believe this is appropriate for all students, not just those who have traditionally enrolled in vocational education (Raizen, 1991).

The Emergence of Tech Prep

Out of this smorgasbord of proposals, tech prep has emerged as a dominant theme. Without question, it can open new doors for many students and be of particular assistance to the "neglected majority" (Parnell, 1985). Its instructional content, which is based on competencies needed to succeed in the evolving marketplace, gives these students the focus previously missing from their educational experience.

As these students receive more instruction in an experiential mode and in context-specific situations, it is almost certain that they will begin to see the practical application of their coursework. And, seeing its utility, they are much more likely to learn the content quickly and retain it longer. When this pedagogical approach is the basis for secondary courses that lead directly into advanced instruction of a similar nature at a cooperating postsecondary institution or in an apprenticeship program, students experience educational success, perhaps for the first time in their lives.

Tech prep exists in many different programmatic configurations in the schools of America today. Most, if not all, of these configurations fit somewhere on a continuum that runs from those that require little or no systemic change to those that mandate (and contribute to) major reform of the educational system of which they are a part (see Figure 1.1).

Many of the practitioners who have designed these configurations claim to have implemented a tech prep *program* in their schools, and in truth, they have. Certainly they have implemented their vision of tech prep, and there is absolutely nothing wrong with any of these configurations. Each one is, more than likely, an improvement upon that which existed earlier in that system and sends a message that local educational leaders are concerned, thinking, and attempting to change.

Nor is there anything wrong with calling these configurations ''programs,'' *in the short-run.* This is true so long as the term ''tech prep program'' connotes the packaging of currently available educational experiences and opportunities in order to provide a more visible career pathway for students, rather than a pre-determined set of activities and expectations imposed upon the local situation. And it is true so long as

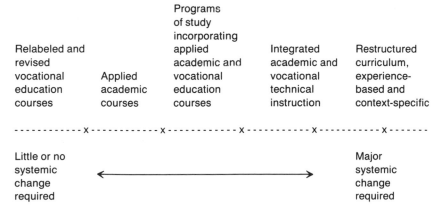

Figure 1.1 *Tech prep continuum of change.*

the package in question is viewed by the system as an interim arrangement, which it will use only until it can do a more effective job for its consumers.

The danger comes when any one of these configurations is viewed as a goal or an end in and of itself, rather than as a step in the right direction. The same type of danger awaits those who view tech prep as a program, rather than as a strategy; they may be tempted to glorify the so-called program and "circle the wagons" in a defensive gesture. Either of these reactions is unfortunate and inappropriate: *the goal of continuous quality improvement in tech prep or any other reform strategy is never reached. It is the distance an organization travels in that direction that is ultimately important, not the phases through which it may pass along the way.*

PITFALLS CONFRONTING TECH PREP

Three major pitfalls (each the antithesis of the systemic improvement of an organization's processes taught by Deming through TQM) loom in the path of the successful implementation of tech prep as a long-term, comprehensive educational reform strategy:

1) The assumption that any specific tech prep programmatic configuration is the goal, rather than a means to a more important end

2) The lack of a conceptual understanding of tech prep to guide its design, implementation, and evaluation as an educational reform process or strategy and its subsequent connection with other educational reform efforts

3) The failure to recognize that the massive systemic change required of the educational establishment will not occur, no matter how effective the tech prep initiative may be, without external support

Without correcting the second deficiency, it is impossible to avoid the first, for these two form a symbiotic relationship. However, even if both these pitfalls are circumvented, the third remains. The systemic reform desired will not occur just because of the changes generated by tech prep, as important as they may be, because systems cannot, working alone, improve themselves. Such improvement ". . . requires profound knowledge as a guide," which, as a rule, ". . . comes from outside and by invitation" (Deming, in process, 82). Tech prep, at its best then, is still an internal educational reform effort, which will succeed to the degree that appropriate external support is generated and maintained.

Negotiating this third pitfall will require dealing initially with the first two. Until the internal dynamics of the reform initiative are understood and mastered by educational practitioners, there is little or nothing for which to gain external support. So although a great deal may be inferred from this book about how to deal with the third, the focus is more on how to avoid pitfalls one and two.

THE DANGERS OF ARTIFICIAL SEPARATION

The first of these pitfalls has its footing in the continuation in many secondary schools, of the historic separation of academic education from any program (in this case, tech prep) that prepares people for work. Nor is this separation restricted to the secondary level; many postsecondary institutions suffer from it as well. In some of these situations, tech prep is seen as simply a variation upon the old vocational education theme. In another example, not only are the tracks that have historically separated academic and vocational education being left intact, but a third track (applied academics) is being built. Regrettably, the cultural dualism against which Dewey (1915) fought is still very much alive.

Admittedly, there is a growing realization that both the academic and technical skills of students must be improved for them to succeed in the workplace. However, seldom does anyone seem to recognize that tech prep is ideally positioned to draw upon the pedagogical and philosophical experience that vocational education has garnered through its seventy-five years of practicing experiential teaching and learning. Nor have there been many attempts to marshall this experience to empower teachers to teach the requisite technical *and* academic skills. The best example of a serious and successful attempt of this nature is found in the work being carried out under the auspices of the Southern Regional Education Board (SREB) (Bottoms and Presson, 1989).

This lack of pedagogical interest in vocational education exists in spite of the fact that those who were most instrumental in drawing up the 1990 Perkins Act (which, in addition to increasing the funding for tech prep, mandated the integration of academic and vocational education) acknowledge the contributions vocational education can make in reforming schools. For example, Jack Jennings, one of the primary authors of that legislation, believes that vocational education motivates students to learn, shows them the practical connection between what they learn in school and the work they will do once they leave school, and places abstract knowledge into the practical context of real-life problems and situations (Jennings, 1991).

Although the author agrees with Jennings and recommends placing the most effective practices of vocational education at the core of tech prep, *this does not mean that tech prep is a revised, updated, or relabeled version of vocational education. Nor does it mean that vocational educators bear the sole responsibility for tech prep.* Either of these misperceptions causes one to fall immediately into the first pitfall mentioned above.

Yet, a review of current tech prep organizational patterns suggests that many local administrators do not understand the complex and sensitive relationship that exists between tech prep and vocational education. Instead, they seem to have a great deal of difficulty comprehending just how tech prep can make use of effective vocational education strategies, without actually becoming the same as traditional vocational education in the process.

For example, in some thirty-eight grants made in 1991 to tech prep consortia in one state, more than 90 percent listed the local director of vocational education as the contact person. It is quite likely that these are also the people who were primarily responsible for tech prep in those districts and consortia. They were certainly *perceived* as those who were most responsible. Indeed, the assumption in most schools, school districts, and postsecondary institutions in this country today is that the primary players in tech prep will be vocational education teachers and administrators, *unless top level administration has made it clear by word and deed that it is a system-wide strategy.*

The assignment of responsibility for tech prep solely to vocational educators is apparently not entirely at their request. In fact, some of their leaders have warned of the dangers inherent in such practices (Belcher, 1991). One has to assume then that these assignments are made by the local district leadership based upon:

1) Their lack of understanding of tech prep as a comprehensive educational reform strategy
2) The system's tradition and inertia (i.e., these kinds of programs have always been assigned to vocational educators)
3) The administrators' belief that only vocational education personnel have the experience necessary to lead tech prep

4) Their unwillingness to accept responsibility for the occupational preparation of their students in the name of the entire school system, rather than just in the name of vocational education

If reasons one, two, or three are the basis for the decision, the situation is relatively easy to correct. If reason four is the determining factor, tech prep is as doomed to failure in that system, as was Dewey's (1915) comprehensive vision of vocational education at the turn of the century.

The problem is not how to devise ways to exclude vocational educators from tech prep; indeed, *they must be involved*. Instead, it is the perception, apparently held by some, that if the funds and the leadership are coming only from vocational education, then the operational definition of tech prep does not extend beyond the historic interests of vocational education, no matter what claims are made to the contrary. When these historic interests are believed to be inconsistent with those of the more academic college preparatory curriculum of the secondary school (the prevailing belief since 1917), the stage is set for increased fragmentation.

Some suggest the problem would be eliminated if tech prep dollars were not allocated as vocational education funds. Although the suggestion may have some merit, it is probably much too simplistic. It is unlikely that a comprehensive vision of tech prep would result from simply changing the designation of the funding, because the inclination to separate is not restricted to vocational educators.

Approaches to tech prep that are comprised solely of applied academic courses and exclude vocational educators are of equal concern. While it is entirely appropriate, and in fact laudable, to introduce courses such as Principles of Technology and Applied Mathematics into the secondary school curriculum, they too should be viewed as first steps in a continuing reformation process, rather than as ends in and of themselves. When these courses are implemented without taking advantage of the experience of appropriate vocational education teachers, their laboratories, and their pedagogy, major opportunities are being missed. These missed opportunities include the possibility of reforming the system, as well as improving the instruction of the targeted students.

The Real Villain

The most likely culprit in this educational pavane is the historic misunderstanding and tension that continues to this day between vocational and academic teachers and instructional leaders. For example, in a recent interview, an automobile mechanics teacher referred to his college preparatory counterparts as "those people who have never had to do a 'real' day's work in their lives." Ironically, but not surprisingly, a high-ranking central office administrator in that same district was heard to say that very same day, "There is no way those vocational teachers are going to get their hands on our Principles of Technology course and mess it up too." These artificial distinctions continue the uneasy "we" *versus* "they" relationship between vocational and academic educators, when the documented common enemy is instructional fragmentation and teacher isolation (Farnham-Diggory, 1990).

One can take the position that Pogo was correct (i.e., "We have found the enemy, and it is us"), or it may be more meaningful to listen to Benjamin Franklin: "In this matter, we [academic and vocational educators] must hang together, or we shall surely hang separately." A third possibility is to recognize that there are no enemies; there are only groups of well-intentioned educators, most of whom have much to offer, but who just don't know how to get their acts together.

NEEDED: A COMMON POINT OF DEPARTURE

Those who develop a tech prep initiative can avoid having it become a separate track at the implementation site. They can also begin to erase the historic separation of vocational and college preparatory (academic) education in their school. Tech prep can be a cohesive force uniting these two rather than reinforcing the walls around either, or creating a third.

To do so, however, will require that both college preparatory teachers and administrators and their vocational education counterparts be involved in the tech prep initiative from the outset. It will also demand their patience, commitment, and goodwill. Most importantly, the participants must be willing to dig deeply into their own pedagogical understandings and philosophies of education, until they arrive at common roots. For "if we are looking for spectacular improvements in learning, they lie, not solely, but importantly in pedagogic [and philosophic understanding and] changes" (Berryman and Bailey, 1992, 114).

One might reasonably ask how such a search could possibly bring together members of two groups that historically have taken opposite positions on many, if not most, significant education issues. Might not such an activity widen the gap instead?

It is true that college preparatory and vocational education sprang from two disparate philosophical mindsets. [It is important to note that these "mindsets" were not the product of isolated intellectual discussions among educators. Instead, they were rooted, as is always the case, in the economic, social, political, and psychological context of the day, which explains why the current mindset, and therefore the educational paradigm, is shifting once again (Lunsford, 1993).] And the debates that raged during the late nineteenth and early twentieth centuries between the advocates of these two educational approaches served primarily to highlight and sharpen their differences. It is also true that the sometimes dramatic disagreements they have experienced during the past seventy-five years have most often been justified more on the basis of those early philosophical distinctions, rather than on present-day realities.

For example, if one analyzes current classroom practice, there is ample evidence that these seventy-five years have seen a gradual movement of both groups toward a more centrist position. College preparatory (academic) instruction has become more pragmatic, while vocational education now promotes theory almost as much as specific skills. It is hypothesized that if teachers from the two fields reflect sufficiently upon their practices, they will discover that they already share many aspects of a common pedagogy and educational philosophy.

The task, therefore, is not to get either or both groups to adopt a new philosophy. Instead, it is to get them to recognize the commonality of what they already believe. They can then begin to act upon these commonalities, rather than upon the differences that were laid down by others at the turn of the century, which are now only clumsy and artificial encumbrances to both groups.

A prerequisite for a successful tech prep initiative is the willingness and ability of the participants to go beneath (or rise above) their areas of instructional expertise until a common ground is reached—whether it be called a goal, purpose, aim, educational theory, principle, pedagogy, or philosophy of education.

This is much more easily said than done. Typically, secondary teachers and postsecondary faculty and staff members have given little, if any, thought to such issues. They will need to be led carefully through a labyrinth of seemingly conflicting theories and beliefs until they begin to recognize that their similarities are indeed greater and far more important than their assumed differences. This can be a difficult, and at times painful, journey. But it is one they must undertake if they are to be anything more than minimally successful in using tech prep as an educational reform strategy.

REACHING A COMMON GROUND

Unfortunately, this journey will get very little guidance or direction from the current knowledge base about tech prep. To reach that common ground, the concepts that can make tech prep most effective must be identified and promulgated. This conceptual foundation is not delineated in any of the tech prep models that have cropped up around the country, nor does the literature offer many clues.

In the absence of such a conceptual foundation, the reference most frequently used by practitioners is Hull and Parnell's (1991) *Tech Prep Associate Degree: A Win/Win Experience*. Although the authors who contributed to that publication provide a great deal of useful information about successful tech prep initiatives, much of it is more promotional than analytical. And few, if any, real questions or criticisms are raised about tech prep itself.

This criticism does not disparage Hull and Parnell's work. Their goals were to raise their readers' level of consciousness about the problem and get them moving along the continuum of change. And there is no question but that they have more than achieved those goals. Nor does it suggest that those who have implemented successful local tech prep initiatives have not based them upon sound concepts. Indeed, they must have – otherwise, they would not have been so successful. And they are acting out these conceptual understandings, including their pedagogy and educational philosophy, through their programmatic activities (Castell, 1964).

It does, however, suggest that the concepts that have guided the tech prep pioneers have remained implicit and are, therefore, subject to many interpretations by those who attempt to follow their lead. The results, all too often, have been attempts to replicate the models without going through the difficult thinking and conceptual struggles that preceded their development.

That there is no extant conceptual foundation for tech prep is not an indictment of the work of these pioneers. All over the country, they have built innovative and effective initiatives against considerable odds. It has not been their intention to design a conceptual framework or foundation prior to beginning their activities. In truth, they have gained great respect from private, political, and educational leaders for doing something that works, rather than merely talking, hypothesizing, philosophizing, or writing about it.

It is not enough, however, just to see these programs work in their original settings and then pursue their replication. At a minimum, those who wish to follow need to ask some very difficult questions of themselves early in the process, preferably well before they visit such a program, for example:

1) What are the most critical educational problems facing my school, school district, and postsecondary institution?

2) What is my school's, school district's, and postsecondary institution's comprehensive plan for addressing these problems?

3) What kind of educational reform activities are my school, school district, and postsecondary institution already undertaking to deal with these problems?

4) What changes will these activities cause in my school, school district, and postsecondary institution, as well as in my consortium's (assuming one has been established) service delivery area?

5) Upon what pedagogical (teaching/learning) principles are these activities built?

6) What are the pedagogical connections between these activities and tech prep?

7) Where will tech prep fit into the comprehensive plan for educational and structural change in my school, school district, and postsecondary institution?

TAKING THE NEXT STEPS

At their best, without a clear conceptual foundation, many of the current tech prep initiatives are likely to end up haphazardly treating symptoms (e.g., high dropout rates, low standardized test scores, poor attendance, and poor job placement rates). As important as these problems are, they are not the real factors (e.g., cultural and educational dualism) that precipitated the difficulty in which American education finds itself. At their worst, when some of the efforts fail (as some surely must), tech prep may lose its current attractiveness and be consigned to the educational junk heap, along with other innovations that had poorly understood conceptual underpinnings (e.g., career education).

If a clear conceptual foundation for tech prep were available, educational leaders could make more intelligent decisions about its design, implementation, and evaluation, as well as when and how to connect it with other educational reform strategies to make their school's, school system's, and postsecondary institution's instructional offerings more consistent with the realities of today and the future and more satisfying to their consumers. The remainder of this book is devoted to constructing that foundation. Chapter 2 describes the process through which it will be built.

Constructing a Conceptual Foundation

FORTUNATELY, constructing a conceptual foundation for tech prep does not begin in a vacuum; the movement is evolving within a changing but observable context. Its configuration is being forged by many factors, including public beliefs and expectations; demographic, political, and socioeconomic pressures; and recent findings about how people learn best, to name but a few. Some of these factors are relatively easy to identify, others are not. Most importantly, there is no apparent pattern to their interaction that practitioners can use as a basis for planning their own initiatives. These factors *can* be identified, and the pattern formed when connections are made between and among them *can* be detected, through an analysis of critical segments of the context, each of which offers a different perspective.

When these analyses are completed, the findings fit together as structural components of a foundation for understanding, designing, and implementing tech prep. This foundation can also support and inform tech prep's future growth and development as an educational reform strategy. Of most significance, it provides educators with guidelines for conceptualizing their own approaches, consistent with the unique requirements of their specific situations. And for those who have already begun the tech prep journey but are not satisfied with their direction or rate of progress, it serves as a basis for reassessing their destination, their current situation, and their process.

Tech prep educators not only need to understand the process described below and implemented in subsequent chapters, but, more importantly, *they need to work through this process for themselves as they plan their specific educational reform initiatives*. If they do, they will be well on their way to making systemic educational improvement. To do less will result in a clear and theoretically sound, but of necessity, generic understanding of tech prep (presented in this book), which stops far short of addressing the unique problems of their school, school district, and postsecondary institution.

For this reason, as each structural component of the foundation is laid, one or more questions about the local situation is presented for which *practitioners must derive their own answers*. Answering these questions will enable them to refine the dimensions of the component under consideration and make it more consistent with the needs of their locality. To help them get involved in and "own" this process, a section entitled "Putting Concepts into Practice," which includes a list of activities suggested for pursuing answers to these local questions, is found at the end of most chapters. Practitioners are urged to use the activities that are applicable to their situation.

CONSTRUCTING THE FOUNDATION

The stages through which the conceptual foundation is built in Chapters 3–11 are described, step-by-step, in the text below. The accompanying figures are designed to help the reader develop an image of the individual structural components that comprise the foundation and visualize the dynamics of their interaction.

Establishing the Boundaries—Precepts and Expectations

A conceptual foundation for tech prep (or any other education reform initiative) must be consistent with the most valid possible description of what the American body politic (in TQM terms, the ultimate customer or consumer) believes about and expects from its public schools (Savary, 1992, 3). These precepts and expectations define the boundaries or perimeter in which practitioners are authorized to operate at any given point in time (see Figure 2.1).

In this complex day and age, identifying these boundaries is not as simple as it might seem. Far too often, practitioners assume that they know what these boundaries are, without giving them sufficient attention. Or they may be listening to only one client group, rather than the community as a whole. On the other hand, they may simply not think about such issues, and even if they do, they may find the parameters of their situation difficult to identify and comprehend.

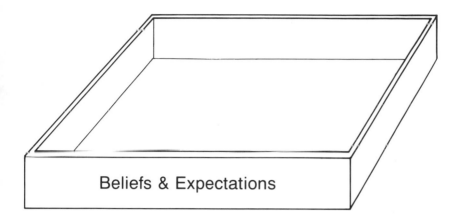

Beliefs & Expectations

Figure 2.1 *Constructing a conceptual foundation for tech prep: defining the boundaries.*

The boundaries of the conceptual foundation for tech prep can begin to be defined by seeking answers to the questions below. As explained earlier, the first of these questions deals with the national (macro) context, the second with the local situation.

What beliefs about (precepts) and expectations of their schools do most Americans seem to hold? What precepts and expectations seem to be held by the customers or consumers of the products and services of my local school, school district, and postsecondary institution?

Once these tentative boundaries have been established, the interaction of other structural components that affect tech prep can be plotted within them. Several of these major components are discussed below. Although attention will be given to all of them, some are more influential than others and will be treated accordingly.

Demographic Indicators

America is changing, rapidly reaching the point where the historic minority groups are approaching majority status in many localities. Simultaneously, increasingly varied immigrant populations are changing traditional cultural perspectives. Other socioeconomic and cultural forces (e.g., single-parent families, an aging population, and the rapid increase of women in the workplace) make Americans different in important ways from citizens of thirty, twenty, and even ten years ago.

Tech prep planners are faced, then, with this second set of questions:

What changes are occurring in the demographic composition of America? What is the effect of these changes on its educational system? What is the effect of the changing demographic characteristics of my school, school district, and postsecondary institution and my community and service area upon our educational offerings?

Answers to these questions will allow the identification and description of the first component to be placed within the boundaries of the conceptual foundation (see Figure 2.2).

Many practitioners already understand some of this critical information. However, all too often, these data are treated as a proposal ''boiler-plate,'' which has little impact on local decision making, and is not thought of again until it is time for the next proposal. For effective educational programming, this information must be internalized and used on a regular basis for continuous systemic improvement.

The Evolving Workplace

As America moves into the twenty-first century, the influence of change in the evolving workplace is being felt in every classroom. No educational activity will escape this pressure, especially not tech prep. Therefore, a description of these changes, one of the more complex features of the foundation (see Figure 2.3), becomes of paramount importance:

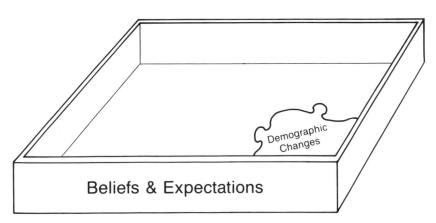

Figure 2.2 *Constructing a conceptual foundation for tech prep: pertinent demographic indicators.*

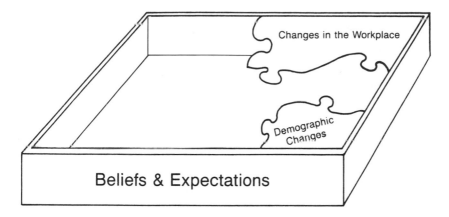

Figure 2.3 *Constructing a conceptual foundation for tech prep: the evolving workplace.*

What are the dynamics of change in the international, national, regional, and local labor markets? What competencies are needed for success in these changing labor markets? How do these competencies differ from those of yesterday and today? Is my local instructional program providing students with these competencies? If not, what changes must we make?

Although more and more practitioners are also recognizing their need to understand the workplace better, some of these data pose problems that are quite perplexing. For example, while it is true that the future bodes well for those who have a technical skill to sell, it is also quite likely, due to the nature of local economies, that the first job for many secondary and postsecondary graduates for years to come will continue to be ''low skill-low pay'' (Berryman, Knuth, and Law, 1992). How is the local practitioner to balance these two contradictory but apparently accurate pieces of information and plan instructional approaches that cover both eventualities?

The best answer seems to be to teach students how to continue to learn in and from that first job, so that it will not become their only job. This, however, requires understanding both the high-tech and low-tech sectors of the labor market. It also requires helping students construct career ladders that lead from one sector to the other, a very complex undertaking. Such a task can present a major problem for many practitioners who, quite understandably, may not be particularly sophisticated in the management and interpretation of labor market statistics.

Unless they are very careful and, for most, unless they seek expert assistance when faced with this and similar situations, many practitioners are likely to get caught up in the corporate and political rhetoric mentioned below and focus only on the much more exciting high-tech data. To do so, however, is to create a completely false future for students in many regions of this country.

Such an inappropriate response is most likely to occur when tech prep has been developed primarily as a knee-jerk reaction to external pressures. If, on the other hand, it is a comprehensive educational improvement strategy, which includes being responsive to the evolving labor market and *much, much more* (the findings of cognitive science presented below confirm this possibility), such a mistake is less likely.

Corporate and Political Influence

When major employment shifts occur, and especially, when the economy suffers, corporate leaders and politicians scramble for solutions, and the public schools immediately come under their scrutiny. This is exactly what happened during the 1980s and early 1990s. More often than not, public schools were identified as *the* problem, and tech prep has been increasingly suggested as *the* solution to those problems. Both of these statements are dangerous generalizations.

While it is reasonable to expect such a reaction from business leaders and politicians, prudent educators will carefully analyze the pressures that build up behind a movement such as tech prep. Those who have developed comprehensive plans for educational change will make these pressures work for well thought-out educational improvement, rather than allow themselves and their schools to be swept along with the tide.

This requires the honest recognition that when politicians and corporate leaders talk about reforming schools, they are acting in their own self-interest, as well as on behalf of schools and students. And while this is entirely appropriate, educators must be able to fit their criticisms and offers of assistance into the educational scheme of things, without abdicating their professional responsibilities.

Answers to the following questions can assist practitioners as they face this task:

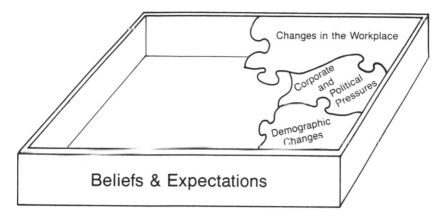

Figure 2.4 *Constructing a conceptual foundation for tech prep: corporate and political pressures.*

What corporate and political pressures are influencing American education? How do these pressures interact? What is the result of these pressures on national, state, and local views about tech prep? How can I use these pressures to effect long-term and positive educational change in my school, school district, and postsecondary institution?

Thus will be developed a third component of the conceptual foundation. Answers to these questions will also suggest the interaction of this component with the demographic and marketplace information already in place (see Figure 2.4).

Recent Research into Effective Instruction

Some who lead tech prep do not appear to be looking beyond themselves and their movement for solutions to the organizational and instructional problems they face. This is a serious mistake, reminiscent of the position taken by many vocational educators over the years.

In truth, much is being learned in other fields that has immediate application to instructional programming in tech prep. For example, the latest research by cognitive scientists teaches that present-day schools may not even be organized in ways that support effective learning. And more and more, it is being discovered that it may well be the schools' pedagogy that is at fault, rather than the content taught in their classes.

(Both of these findings are reminiscent of Deming's research on business and industrial organization.) Findings such as these add a great deal of information and understanding to the repertoire of tech prep planners and must be built into their conceptual foundation.

The following questions point the way (see Figure 2.5):

> What does the latest research teach about the process of effective teaching and learning? How can these findings be built into a local tech prep initiative? What other instructional reform initiatives are taking place in my school, school district, and postsecondary institution? Upon what pedagogical (teaching/learning) premises are they built? What are the pedagogical connections between these activities and our vision of tech prep?

Intriguing corollaries between education and work are also being discovered. The restructured workplace and the restructured school are becoming more alike, and the practices that make for effective learning seem to be akin to those that make for effectiveness on the job (Berryman and Bailey, 1992). This presents an opportunity for tech prep practitioners to make a unique contribution. This is especially true for those whose initiative is integrated into a comprehensive educational improvement process (e.g., TQE). They may discover that they can serve as conduits for sharing examples of successful restructuring in both directions (i.e., from the school to the workplace as well as from the workplace to the school).

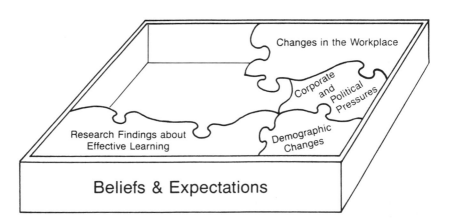

Figure 2.5 *Constructing a conceptual foundation for tech prep: research findings about effective learning.*

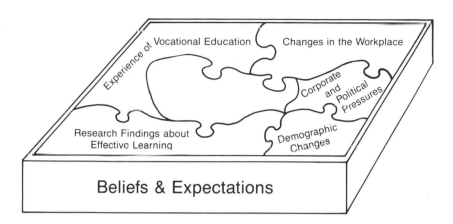

Figure 2.6 *Constructing a conceptual foundation for tech prep: the experience of vocational education.*

The Experience of Vocational Education

If America's schools and their instructional programs are out of step with effective learning theory, as cognitive scientists and others suggest, then a major realignment of current pedagogical practices is in order. Does this mean that educators must start over from the very beginning? Or is there sufficient experience in any current or historic approach from which lessons can be learned and upon which new instructional efforts can be built? If the latter is a possibility, a great deal of time and other resources may be saved. Vocational education is hypothesized to be one such major experience base.

A sixth set of questions becomes important at this stage in the construction of the conceptual foundation (see Figure 2.6):

> What is vocational education's experience in American education and with this more effective pedagogy? What lessons can be learned from this experience that will assist in restructuring schools? Is such an experience base available in my school, school district, and postsecondary institution? If so, how can we take advantage of this experience?

Those who offer tech prep as an answer to the nation's need for highly skilled employees, well-grounded in appropriate theory and concepts, can learn a great deal from the history of vocational education. *Tech prep practitioners need not repeat the mistakes made in the past by vocational educators, but they likely will unless they learn from those mistakes.*

The Pedagogy and Philosophy of Effective Tech Prep

As important as they are, the components of the foundation that will have been put in place to this point are still not likely to be of much help to teachers who feel isolated within a system that seems designed to preclude their working together as a team (a prerequisite of TQE). All teachers need help in breaking out of this isolation, whatever its cause and wherever it exists. It is especially important for college preparatory (academic) and vocational education teachers who are involved in tech prep to learn to cooperate across the artificial instructional lines that have historically divided them. "Removing such barriers is a key role of the TQM-enlightened manager" (Lunsford, 1993).

Such interaction will require their developing a neutral ground or common playing field upon which they can connect. This in turn can come about only by their identifying consistent pedagogical principles and a reasonably clear belief structure or philosophy to which all parties generally agree. They can then stand, side-by-side as it were, on this playing field as they build collaborative activities from their distinctive vantage points.

The component that will now be developed and placed at the center of the conceptual foundation (i.e., its philosophical core), is more complex than the first six. For that reason, it requires more description and explanation.

The Practical Value of Pedagogy and Philosophy

Most educators will accept the necessity of developing pedagogical principles more readily than they will the idea of working out their educational philosophy. The word "philosophy" causes the eyes of many to glaze over. Perhaps memories come to mind of the seemingly useless task of writing a statement of philosophy for a visit from a regional accrediting agency, which was most likely stored in the file until their next visit. In this case, something much more meaningful, practical, and valuable is being sought.

But still, why bother? Isn't it really a waste of time? In response, a quotation from John Gardner is apropos:

> An excellent plumber is infinitely more admirable than an incompetent philosopher. The society which scorns excellence in plumbing because plumbing is a humble activity and tolerates shoddiness in philosophy

because it is an exalted activity will have neither good plumbing nor good philosophy. Neither its pipes nor its theories will hold water. (Gardner, 1985, 24)

This quotation is often used to illustrate the value of plumbing (and other trades), a noteworthy point. However, the operative words are "excellence" and "shoddiness," not "plumber" and "philosopher." Gardner was not maligning philosophy. Instead, his warning concerned shoddiness in either activity. It is important for both pipes *and* theories to hold water. *In short, analyzing one's philosophical mindset is as hard-headed, practical, and sense-making an activity as is connecting pipe.*

On the other hand, there is nothing noble in philosophical pursuits, if one merely wishes ". . . to hang out one's intellectual shingle; . . . indeed, there is a tendency to stop thinking about things once you have found your own little 'ism' " (Morris, 1961, 472). So how can a philosophical approach help practitioners deal with the current dilemma? What do philosophers do that is practical and useful? How can such an approach strengthen tech prep initiatives?

Philosophy has three main functions: the descriptive, the normative, and the analytic (Wingo, 1974). Tech prep has no need for developing a *descriptive* philosophy of education from parent philosophies. Nor does it appear timely (later, perhaps) or appropriate to suggest just what a *normative* philosophy for tech prep should be. Instead, the task is to identify the philosophy or philosophies that already exist, albeit implicitly for the most part, in the minds and subsequent actions of successful tech prep practitioners. The *analytic* philosophical approach can facilitate this task:

When people have a choice, they must have some reason for deciding to do one thing instead of another, and behind every set of school policies, which are more or less formalized, and organized statements for action stands some set of accepted ideas and ideals.

It would appear that one of the proper functions of [educational philosophy] would be to inquire into [these] sets of educational ideas and ideals, discover what they are, subject them to critical scrutiny, test them for logical consistency, and judge their adequacy. (Wingo, 1974, 16)

It can be safely asserted that persons who have been in education for any length of time have a philosophy of education guiding their actions. It is that innate set of presuppositions that enables one to make decisions, to choose between x and y, and formulate strategies for program implementation:

Your philosophy, no matter who you are or what you do, consists of those ultimate principles and ultimate presuppositions which, whether you know it or not, are operative in your behavior. . . . is it better to leave them alone, better not to dig them up and expose them to light of conscious awareness? Perhaps so, provided they are not creating debilitating strains in the mind which they structure, provided the activity which they facilitate is not encountering a too radical frustration. . . . (Castell, 1964, 1–2)

In some instances, tech prep is encountering just such a "radical frustration" of its central theme and ultimate power as an educational reform strategy. This is occurring most often where it is viewed as *only* another program or track within the secondary and postsecondary curriculum or as an end in and of itself, rather than as a means to a larger end. The fact that those who are making these decisions do not recognize the "debilitating strains" or the "radical frustration" of the concept such decisions cause makes it no less a problem. In truth, their lack of perception exacerbates the seriousness of the situation.

[It must be pointed out once again that the emergence of a specific programmatic configuration at the local level, *in the short run*, is not inappropriate, so long as there continues to be movement toward the ultimate union of the concepts of effective academic and vocational education under the aegis of the tech prep initiative. But if the particular configuration takes on the form of an achieved goal and the wagons are circled to protect it, tech prep's potential as a reform strategy in that system will not be reached. However, even in these cases where the power of tech prep will be severely limited, local practitioners should be commended *because the configuration they have chosen may be far more progressive than their having done nothing* (Lunsford, 1993)].

How, then, does one conduct an analysis of the type Castell and Wingo advocate? Optimally, one would get inside the heads of those who run successful tech prep initiatives and analyze their actions as well as their words. However, there is a more efficient way to begin, which will provide partial answers, and in the long run, shorten the process. This calls for using the best practices of vocational education as a proxy for tech prep.

The Best Practices of Vocational Education as Proxy

At this point, the reader may well say, "Wait a minute. You've already convinced me that tech prep is not the same thing as vocational education." While that is true, it has also been argued (and will be subsequently demonstrated) that the best practices of vocational education embody the pedagogical principles and educational philosophy that are essential to the success of tech prep. In other words, *although tech prep is much more than vocational education, incorporating the best of the latter is essential to the success of the former.* To walk this narrow line of distinction is one of the most important and difficult tasks facing tech prep educators.

Vocational education has existed in the public schools for seventy-five years. Admittedly, it has experienced many problems. Conversely, many of its concepts and programs have exhibited a remarkable degree of resilience through the good times and the not-so-good times. Critics may charge that this is more a political than a pedagogical or philosophical phenomenon, but it is much more likely that the consistent beliefs of its supporters and their commitment to similar goals is the real reason. As vague as these beliefs and goals may often seem, even to vocational educators themselves, the longevity of many of their programmatic strategies attests to the strength of their pedagogical principles and philosophical roots.

The initial task then, is to identify and analyze the best practices of vocational education. ''Best practices'' are defined as major strategies, activities, and approaches of vocational education that open up the career options of students, teach them theory as well as specific skills, and motivate them to learn. These practices will then be used as lenses through which to view the pedagogical principles and philosophical beliefs that foster them.

Is this pedagogy and philosophy worth the time and energy it will take for its explication? According to Hruska (1974, 56), it is, for:

> Within [vocational education's] ethos of involvement, interest, creativity, self-expression, and skill development is the framework for an educational idea that is consistent with both rigorous ideals and contemporary learning theory.

Inferring a Pedagogy and an Educational Philosophy

How then, does one explicate that ''framework for an educational idea?'' Castell (1964) recommended tracking down a principle or premise through repeated applications of the interrogative ''Why?'' to any assertion one is prepared to authorize or any stand one is willing to take. The process used in this book is based upon that approach and is illustrated in Figure 2.7. Its specific steps include:

1) Identifying vocational education strategies, activities, and approaches that have been successful in increasing the career options of students, teaching them theory as well as specific skills, and motivating them to learn

2) Repeatedly asking the question: "Why has vocational education historically supported these practices with so much enthusiasm?"

3) Inferring answers based upon a limited review of the literature, which emerge as premises of vocational education

4) Organizing these premises, using a model developed by William Frankena (1966), to determine the relationship of each premise to all the others

5) Offering the resulting statement as a tentative philosophy of education (including its inherent pedagogy) that supports and guides the best practices of vocational education

How the Process Works

The following example demonstrates how this inferential process works. It is relatively easy to identify cooperative education as a best practice of vocational education (i.e., it meets all the necessary criteria). However, to say that one believes in cooperative education is not a statement of one's educational philosophy. Nor does it offer specific pedagogical handles for the practitioner to grasp.

The question is, "*Why* has vocational education supported cooperative education so strongly and practiced it as an instructional strategy for so many years?" It is hypothesized that vocational educators must share some very specific beliefs about such things as the educational process, teaching, learning, and students that lead them to value this particular instructional strategy. If this is true, what are those beliefs?

Upon a careful review of selected portions of the vocational education literature, one is able to infer the following premises, which those who value and practice cooperative education hold to be true:

1) Education is bound neither by geography nor time.

2) Students learn through all their experiences, not only those that occur within the walls of a classroom.

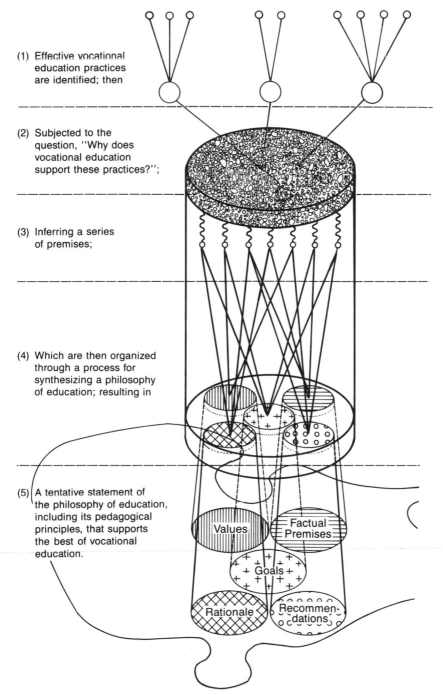

(1) Effective vocational
    education practices
    are identified; then

(2) Subjected to the
    question, "Why does
    vocational education
    support these practices?";

(3) Inferring a series
    of premises;

(4) Which are then organized
    through a process for
    synthesizing a philosophy
    of education; resulting in

(5) A tentative statement of
    the philosophy of education,
    including its pedagogical
    principles, that supports
    the best of vocational
    education.

Values

Factual
Premises

Goals

Rationale

Recommen-
dations

Figure 2.7 *Constructing a conceptual foundation for tech prep: inferring a
pedagogy and educational philosophy for vocational education.*

3) The most effective environment for learning is one that is as true-to-life as possible for the student.

4) Many persons, in addition to baccalaureate-degreed teachers, are capable of providing instruction to student-workers.

For vocational educators to offer these kinds of belief statements to their college preparatory counterparts in explanation of who they are and what they are about is very different from and much more effective than continuing to rely upon their practices as their only descriptors. And with the enunciation of these statements, the building of the common playing field has begun.

The importance of inductively inferring a philosophical statement from specific practices is fourfold:

1) Each pedagogical principle and belief statement can be traced to a specific practice(s).

2) Practices that appear to be inconsistent with the philosophical base can be questioned.

3) New practices can be developed that are consistent with that base.

4) A manageable technique is provided, which teachers and others can use to discover, analyze, and refine their own pedagogical principles and philosophies of education.

On the other hand, such an approach is not without its problems. As Miller (1985) acknowledged, remaining completely objective while inferring these premises is not even a remote possibility. The practices chosen, the supporting documentation, and the inferences drawn are heavily influenced by the author's biases. However, since this process focuses on what leading vocational educators, as well as trusted advocates and friendly critics, have said about vocational education, the inferences are believed to comprise a reasonable approximation of the beliefs of the majority of those who call themselves vocational educators.

A problem still remains. Each of the premises inferred through this process stands alone. In addition, each may be philosophically different from its counterparts in important ways. Some are statements of theory, some are ideological expressions, and some are normative statements, while others are goals or pedagogical recommendations. Therefore, the eventual distillation of approximately 100 premises that takes place in Chapter 9 does not, in and of itself, offer a rational organization of these premises into a statement of educational philosophy.

To provide the necessary organization, Frankena's (1966) model for analyzing (taking apart) a philosophy is adapted to synthesize (put together) the desired statement. The primary value of the model is that it provides a systematic method for beginning to discriminate among the individual premises and, operating somewhat like a template, allows the tentative positioning of each in relationship to the others. Once the premises are placed into this framework, a fairly crude statement of educational philosophy becomes apparent. *In the long run, this statement will need to be analyzed carefully through more academically acceptable philosophical approaches to test its validity. However, as a beginning point, it is a definite improvement upon the current situation.*

Completing the Conceptual Foundation

The next step is to edit the statement so that it speaks to tech prep rather than just to vocational education. If tech prep is more than vocational education, and if it is truly an educational reform strategy that affects all of education, then its philosophical and pedagogical core must be more inclusive than the statement generated in the step described above. This is done through a careful review and revision, editing words and phrases that speak only to or about vocational education and vocational educators, while taking a great deal of care to preserve the fundamental integrity of the original statement (i.e., its footing in and connections with real-life, effective educational practices).

When this edited version of the philosophical statement (which includes its inherent pedagogical principles) is placed at the center of the conceptual foundation (see Figure 2.8), one of the major tasks of this book will near completion. Standing upon this foundation, practitioners can see more clearly and comprehend more fully the complexities of tech prep as it currently exists.

BUILDING UPON THE FOUNDATION

From the outset, the concern has been that some local decision makers appear to be implementing tech prep without a great deal of understanding of its conceptual base and in a rather haphazard manner. Nor does there seem to be anything available to help them to do differently. As stated above, when complete, this conceptual foundation provides

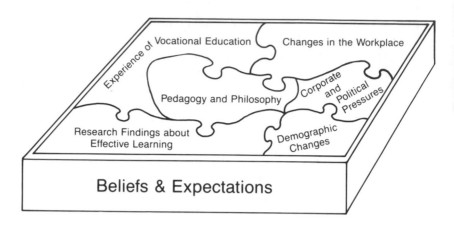

Figure 2.8 *Constructing a conceptual foundation for tech prep: completing the foundation.*

them with a sound base from which to take the first steps to deal with this problem.

However, the more important goal is to help practitioners construct effective approaches specific to their unique situations. Developing a methodology for understanding tech prep retroactively may be a fine scholarly exercise, but the value of this understanding is its usefulness to practitioners as they design and build new initiatives.

By working through the construction of this foundation and internalizing it by digging deeply for answers to questions raised about their local situation, practitioners will be better prepared to conceptualize approaches that fit their specific needs, while selectively and intelligently incorporating elements from other locations. They will also be able to understand why certain aspects of their approach may or may not be as effective as they should be and respond accordingly. Said another way, this conceptual foundation has been designed so that local program designers can use its structural components as building blocks with which to construct their own approaches to tech prep.

In addition, this approach brings practitioners face-to-face with the role of tech prep in the larger picture of school reform. They are compelled to recognize that they are managing an educational reform strategy that draws upon and relates to every other aspect of the social, economic, demographic, and educational paradigm in which it operates. As a result, they will be more aware of the need for and possibilities of connecting tech prep with other reform efforts in their school, school district, and postsecondary institution in a holistic approach to improving education. And in the final analysis, they will be better able to manage the change process, rather than run willy-nilly in a futile attempt to catch up with or escape it.

Having described and explained the process through which the conceptual foundation for tech prep will be built, Chapter 3 begins its construction.

What Americans Believe about and Expect from Their Schools

THE first step in constructing the foundation for tech prep is to define its perimeter. This is done by establishing the national (macro) and local boundaries of permissible educational activity. Just how far will the American public (the ultimate customer or consumer) allow the schools to go, and what do they expect of them in the process?

THE NATIONAL BOUNDARIES OF PERMISSIBLE EDUCATIONAL ACTIVITY

As a nation, America has established some very specific beliefs about and expectations of its public schools. These outer boundaries of permissible educational activity can be discerned through the following question (see Figure 3.1):

What kinds of beliefs about (precepts) and expectations of their schools do most Americans seem to hold at this point in time?

Although Lunsford (1993) warns against fixating upon such boundaries, particularly in their consumer expectation dimension, which he believes may be quite transitory, he agrees that it can be beneficial to conduct consumer research on the topic. Ultimately, he suggests that the primary purpose of such research should be to establish an organization's "leap beyond the known," so that consumer expectations will not only be met, but may be exceeded.

Meeting expectations may confirm quality, but exceeding them extends quality, redefines it, and gives competitive advantage. In education, meeting expectations is training, exceeding expectations builds a love of learning and [possibly] wisdom. (Lunsford, 1993)

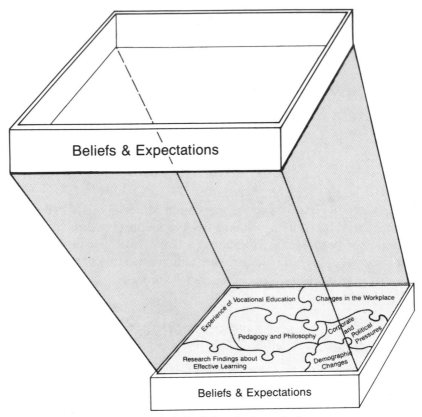

Beliefs & Expectations

Experience of Vocational Education

Changes in the Workplace

Pedagogy and Philosophy

Corporate and Political Pressures

Research Findings about Effective Learning

Demographic Changes

Beliefs & Expectations

Figure 3.1 Defining the boundaries.

These important and legitimate concerns notwithstanding, it is important for tech prep practitioners to get as clear a fix as possible on these beliefs and expectations.

Voices from an Earlier Era

Once the states took seriously their constitutional responsibilities to educate their citizens, most Americans have seemed to hold a fairly consistent set of beliefs about and expectations of their schools. For example, they have always placed a great deal of faith in things that are tangible and practical: "If education is not useful, what is it? . . . Of course, education should be useful, whatever your aim in life. It is useful, because understanding is useful" (Whitehead, 1967, 265). Likewise, they ". . . expected education to prepare for life—by which [they] meant increasingly, jobs and professions" (Commager, 1950, 10).

Perhaps the most formal (and familiar) statement of these beliefs and expectations is found in the so-called Seven Cardinal Principles of Education. These principles were developed in 1918 by the National Education Association's (NEA) Commission on Reorganizing Secondary Education, which recommended that *schools offer instruction in 1) health, 2) command of fundamental processes, 3) worthy home membership, 4) vocation, 5) citizenship, 6) worthy use of leisure time, and 7) ethical character* (Wirth, 1972).

In 1938, the Educational Policies Commission of the NEA proposed the following objectives for education (which resemble the "outcomes of significance" currently being touted under outcome-based education):

1) *Self-Realization*, which included developing the inquiring mind, gaining proficiency in speaking, reading, writing, and the use of numbers in solving problems, acquiring health habits, and the like

2) *Human Relationships*, which included developing respect for humanity, friendships, cooperation, courtesy, appreciation of the home, conservation of the home, and democracy in the home

3) *Economic Efficiency*, which included developing abilities and/or understandings in occupational information, occupational choice, occupational efficiency, occupational adjustment, occupational appreciation, consumer judgment, and buyer efficiency

4) *Civic Responsibility*, which included developing desirable attitudes toward social justice, social activity, social understanding, critical judgment, tolerance, social applications of science, world citizenship, law observance, economic literacy, political citizenship, and devotion to democracy (Klaurens, 1975, 314).

More Recent Declarations

In 1975, when representatives of selected businesses and industries were presented with thirteen educational goals, they ranked them in the following priority order (Klaurens, 1975, 316—317):

1) Fundamental learning skills—reading, writing, and math
2) Critical thinking skills
3) Interpersonal relations skills

4) Career education and occupational competence
5) Self-discipline
6) Individual values
7) Citizenship and political understanding
8) Self-realization
9) Family life and human sexuality
10) Cultural appreciation
11) Economic understanding
12) Physical health
13) Physical environment

These goals were actually more of an extension than a revision of the earlier Cardinal Principles, which evidently have stood the test of time. For, as late as 1976, when a national conference was held to review the adequacy and efficacy of these original principles, conferees reaffirmed their centrality to education. Furthermore, they suggested that secondary schools should continue to build upon the Cardinal Principles, so that their instructional emphasis might be even more meaningful to students of the 1970s. In summary, they declared the primary purpose of American secondary schools to be one of enabling students to participate *advantageously* in their society, which can be interpreted as a rather pragmatic position (Patton, 1976).

During the turbulent 1980s, it may have seemed that any consistency in Americans' beliefs and expectations regarding education was a thing of the past. However, as was reported in Chapter 1 (see p. 5), when the Northeast Regional Exchange reviewed a representative sample of the major critical studies of the period, they discovered an amazing consistency in the precepts underlying their specific recommendations (NEREX, 1985, 56).

National Education Goals (circa 1990)

As the 1980s drew to a close, President George Bush hosted an Education Summit in Charlottesville, Virginia, at which goals for American education were enunciated once again. These goals specified that, by the year 2000 (National Educational Goals Panel, 1991, 2):

• All children in America will start school ready to learn.

- The high school graduation rate will increase to at least 90 percent
- American students will leave grades four, eight, and twelve having demonstrated competency in challenging subject matter including English, mathematics, science, history, and geography; and every school in America will ensure that all students learn to use their minds well, so they may be prepared for responsible citizenship, further learning, and productive employment in our modern economy.
- U.S. students will be first in the world in science and mathematics achievement.
- Every adult American will be literate and will possess the knowledge and skills necessary to compete in a global economy and exercise the rights and responsibilities of citizenship.
- Every school in America will be free of drugs and violence and will offer a disciplined environment conducive to learning.

Although derived heavily from political as well as educational agenda, these goals seemed to be accepted nationwide by the general population as legitimate statements of their own beliefs and expectations. At least no one, except an occasional educator, took issue with them, although that appears to be changing somewhat. It is likely, however, that "Deming would attack these goals, declaring them to be too narrow and numerically based" (Lunsford, 1993).

A Synthesis of Goals and Expectations

When one reviews even this brief history of the goals and expectations established by Americans for their public schools, a fairly clear picture begins to emerge, *although there are many more diversities and complexities inherent in several of these expectations than ever before.* For example, while Americans believe education should perpetuate the cultural heritage, they can't seem to agree on which heritage.

Nevertheless, it can be said with a reasonable amount of confidence that most Americans expect the following from their schools:

1) *Education should be useful and practical.* Americans still pride themselves on being hard-headed Yankee traders. If something in their culture seems to have no purpose beyond itself, it is usually suspect. Most believe education should enable individuals to ac-

complish useful tasks and attain practical goals, including getting, holding, and progressing in a good job, which would otherwise have been beyond their reach. This trend toward utility has shown itself increasingly over the past ten years and can be expected to accelerate in the future. However, caution is advised against adopting utilitarianism as the sole purpose of education for several reasons, not the least of which is that utility may be more an individual perception than a common and concrete reality.

2) *Education should preserve and perpetuate the cultural heritage.* Originally, the teaching and transmission of American culture seemed to be rather simple, focusing mainly on the explication of America's Northern European roots. Recently it has become much more complicated, as Americans have struggled with whether this country is truly a "melting pot" or more a "smorgasbord" of racial and ethnic cultures. These multiple expectations show their strength and diversity in requests for multi-cultural emphasis in all courses, African-American courses, and simultaneously, courses that promote patriotism, an understanding of the Judeo-Christian roots of American government, and respect for the flag.

3) *Education should promote democracy and good citizenship.* This is being heard more and more as crime rates soar and more drugs and guns are brought to school. The lack of understanding of specific governmental structures and functions by high school graduates and their apparent lack of interest in their rights and responsibilities to register and vote are additional concerns.

4) *Education should promote good health habits.* There was also a time when this expectation, like that relating to cultural heritage, was not particularly controversial. Now it encompasses sex education, AIDS education, alcohol, drugs, and many other complex and sensitive issues.

5) *Education should provide skills for securing employment.* As the economy has tightened its grip on more and more families, the importance of every person possessing the skills necessary to earn a decent living has become increasingly clear. The massive numbers of females, minorities, and immigrants who have entered the labor market have exacerbated the situation. And fierce competition in the international marketplace has fanned the embers of this expectation into a veritable firestorm.

6) *Education should contribute to the national defense.* Even as the

de-escalation of tension between the Superpowers progresses, the need for a strong defense remains high on America's agenda. This time, the system is likely to be built more upon technology than manpower (e.g., the hotly debated ''Star Wars'' initiative). Such mechanisms will require a highly educated and technologically literate military and civilian workforce to build and maintain them.

7) *Education should be responsive to citizens' economic and social needs.* Recent riots in major urban centers have called dramatic attention, once again, to the plight of many Americans who are culturally different, as well as educationally and economically deprived. Schools can expect to be asked to do even more to alleviate these situations as such pressures mount.

8) *Education should contribute to leisure time enjoyment.* Even though recent data suggest that Americans are working more hours rather than fewer as anticipated just a few short years ago, this demand is still felt through calls for individual skill development in such areas as sports, crafts, and self-improvement.

9) *Education should respond to the needs of adults.* To witness this phenomenon, one need only review the rapid increase in enrollment in adult education programs of all kinds. This demand will increase as the graying of America continues and as more and more people truly become lifelong learners.

10) *Education should be fiscally realistic and educators should be held accountable.* Whatever goals are sought by education, no matter how useful or practical, they must be pursued within the limits of fiscal reality. Beginning in California, the push for accountability has swept the nation. Never again will educators have the luxury of not having to justify every dime spent and, more importantly, every organizational and instructional action proposed.

ESTABLISHING THE DIMENSIONS OF THE LOCAL SITUATION

The foregoing beliefs and expectations outline the national dimensions of the conceptual foundation. However, it is only through answering the question below that local practitioners will be able to determine if these boundaries are consistent with the unique demands of their local situation, or if specific modifications are required:

What kinds of precepts and expectations of education are held by the customers or consumers of the products or services of my local school, school district, and postsecondary institution?

[Although many in education may be uncomfortable with this marketplace terminology, they would be well-advised to learn to deal with it. In the language of TQM, the customer or consumer is simply ". . . someone or something that uses the product of your work" (Savary, 1992, 11) and no money need change hands for there to be such a relationship. Educators must come to understand just who their particular customers and consumers are and what they want, need, and, in this case, will sanction as legitimate.]

Total quality education (TQE) teaches that most of those involved in education will be either a provider or a consumer of the system's product or service, depending upon their perspective at the moment (Savary, 1992). In this case, the question has to do with the expectation of these consumers in the aggregate (i.e., the entire local client system being served by the school, school district, and postsecondary institution). This includes, but may not be limited to, the following groups:

- students
- parents
- teachers
- potential employers
- educational administrators (school and district level)
- members of boards of education and boards of trustees
- county commissioners (or members of a similar local governmental body)
- taxpayers (private and corporate)
- educational interest groups (special education parents, Head Start supporters, etc.)
- local legislative members
- race relations groups (e.g., NAACP)
- others whose needs and wishes have a direct bearing upon instructional programming

Educational leaders need to find out, as nearly as is possible, just what expectations their client groups hold for the local system and what activities they will and will not sanction as the schools attempt to meet those expectations. The results may prove to be consistent with the national boundaries drawn above, or they may require a minor (or, in rare cases, major) redrawing of those borders.

In either case, it is imperative to find out just where local clients or customers seem to stand on this first, and ultimately most important, component of the conceptual foundation. For whatever the local boundaries may be, *they will include the goals or aims of the school, school district, and postsecondary institution. And without a clear statement of goals or aims, no progress is possible* (Deming, 1986).

Putting Concepts into Practice: Collecting Information about Local Beliefs and Expectations

As practitioners define the specific boundaries of their local situation, they may wish to use some of the activities listed below to collect the necessary information, or they may choose to design their own approaches. The methodology they choose is not particularly important. What is important is that they get useful information and that they use it to establish and continually confirm or revise their assessment of their system's specific boundaries for permissible educational activity, especially that which portends change.

There is one primary rule that covers the collection of this and all other information for inclusion in the foundation: *never ask your clients for information until you are very sure that it is not already available to you.* Activities 1 – 3 apply to all information collection activities and can help practitioners discover what is available.

1) Review carefully the information in the files of your school, school district, and postsecondary institution. If the required information is available, assemble it, review it carefully (get others whom you trust to assist you), revise it as necessary, and rewrite it in an appropriate format.

2) Check with administrators of other educational reform initiatives (e.g., TQE or TQM projects, and other, more traditional programs in your school, school district, and postsecondary institution) to see if they have any of the necessary information.

3) Check with administrators in other schools in the district, other nearby districts, and neighboring postsecondary institutions to determine if the information you need is available at any of those sites.

In this case, if the information is not available from these sources:

4) Conduct mail surveys of a representative sample of consumers,

using an open-ended format (e.g., ''What do you think the aims, goals, and purposes of this school, school system, and postsecondary institution should be?'') or ask your respondents to prioritize a list of purposes that you provide to them.

5) Conduct personal (door-to-door) surveys of a representative sample of your consumers, using either of the formats suggested above. Student service clubs, vocational student organizations, PTAs, and other similar groups may be willing to provide assistance in this task.

6) Contract for (or conduct yourself) a telephone survey of a representative sample of consumers, using either of the formats suggested above.

7) Poll the readers of local newspapers, using either of the formats suggested above, regarding their preferences.

8) Conduct community meetings to determine the thinking of your consumers.

9) Conduct an electronic ''town meeting'' through local cable channels.

10) Survey all students above a selected age (or grade level) at school.

11) Secure the assistance of local churches in surveying their congregations, youth and adults alike.

12) Conduct radio talk shows on the topic.

13) Ask the local utility companies to include a survey form with their monthly bills.

14) Ask local employers to include a survey form with their employees' paychecks.

15) Ask the local Chamber(s) of Commerce to survey its members.

16) Place survey forms in local business and industry newsletters.

17) Contract with a third party to determine the expectations of your consumers separately or as part of a larger study that includes other components of the conceptual foundation.

18) If a major university is nearby, contact appropriate department heads (e.g., social sciences, geography, education, etc.) to see if a graduate student(s) can collect the information for you as part of a research project.

When collected, this information should be electronically stored for easy access and analysis. This analysis will be time consuming and should be approached by top management as a serious exercise. Outside professional assistance may be necessary. Once the tentative findings are formulated, they should be shared with the appropriate policy making board(s), seeking active and informed input. After sufficient and appropriate interaction, top administrators should present a draft statement of the system's goals to the board for its review, revision (if necessary), and adoption.

SHARING THE BELIEFS AND EXPECTATIONS WITH CONSUMERS

Once the local boundaries begin to become clear, this information should be shared with local consumers through a variety of approaches. These precepts and expectations should also be used as criteria against which planned activities are compared to establish their legitimacy as the tech prep initiative goes forward.

Remembering Lunsford's (1993) admonition, local practitioners need to recognize that it is not sufficient to identify these boundaries once and assume they will hold for an indefinite period. Even though precepts and expectations tend to change more slowly than do other parts of the conceptual foundation, they still require review, confirmation, and/or modification on a regular basis.

FILLING IN THE BOUNDARIES

A tentative outline of what most Americans believe about and expect of their schools has now been sketched. However, educators are never given free rein to do as they choose to bring about these expectations. Instead, a multitude of pressures, some of which may be inconsistent and, at times, conflicting, influence educational policy making within these boundaries. If one is to implement a comprehensive tech prep initiative successfully, these pressures need to be identified and analyzed. The most prominent of these pressures (i.e., demographic changes, the evolving workplace, and corporate and political influences) are reviewed in the next three chapters.

Demographic Indications of Change[2]

SINCE tech prep is designed to meet the educational and employability needs of students, it is important to see the educational system from their viewpoint. And quite naturally, their perspectives are shaped by their socioeconomic and cultural backgrounds (i.e., who and what they are, and what "baggage" they bring with them to the schoolhouse door). Demographic factors, therefore, comprise the first component to be placed inside the boundaries of the conceptual foundation (see Figure 4.1).

No attempt is made to present sufficient data to paint a comprehensive profile of the United States or its regions. This is not a demographic treatise, and these data change. Most importantly, this information (in regularly updated formats) can be readily accessed by practitioners, in hard copy and electronically. Instead, attention is given to several key indicators and subsequent analyses of these data that illustrate the dramatic effect demographic changes are having on education and educational policy making. Suggestions are made in the section "Putting Concepts into Practice" for securing the necessary information to adjust these data to local situations. A similar approach is used in subsequent chapters for the other components.

THE CHANGING FACE OF AMERICA

Hodgkinson, the dominant authority on the integration of demographic and educational information, put the following simple, yet

[2]Much of the information in this chapter is taken from the work of Harold L. Hodgkinson (1985, 1989, 1992), which, in turn, he based upon and documented with extensive cultural, demographic, economic, and educational studies, reports, and data bases.

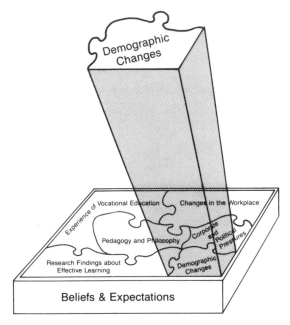

Figure 4.1 Identifying pertinent demographic indicators.

profound, premise before his readers: ''. . . changes in the composition
of the group moving through the educational system will change the
system faster than anything else except nuclear war'' (1985, 1). Educational systems can therefore be understood best as people in motion. And
a study of their characteristics can provide important insights to tech prep
planners faced with the following questions:

> *What changes are occurring in the demographic composition of America?*
> *What is the effect of these changes on its educational system?*

Overall Growth

The population of the United States increased by 22.1 million persons
during the ten years prior to the most recent census, reaching a total of
248.7 million citizens (Hodgkinson, 1992). Table 4.1 shows the 1990
United States population by race and ethnicity, both in total number and
as a percent of the total population. While this 9.8 percent increase in
the population for the decade will affect all of American society, the real
story for education is not told in these figures. Nor is it fully evident even

Table 4.1. U.S. Population by Race and Ethnicity—1990.

	Number	Percent of Population
Total U.S.	248,710,000	100.0
White, non-Hispanic	187,137,000	75.2
Black*	29,986,000	12.1
Native American, Eskimo, Aleut*	1,959,000	0.8
Asian or Pacific Islander	7,274,000	2.9
Hispanic (of any race)	22,354,000	9.0

*Includes a small number of Hispanics.
Source: U.S. Bureau of the Census. Reproduced with permission of the Institute for Educational Leadership, Inc.

in the racial and ethnic percentages of that total population. Instead, it is revealed most clearly through the disparate growth rates among the various racial and ethnic groups.

Differential Birth Rates

Some groups simply have more children than others, and therefore, their percentage of future generations of students will increase over time. Blacks, for example, have an average birth rate of 2.4 children per female, and Mexican-American females average 2.9 children, while Cubans and whites average 1.3 and 1.7 children, respectively (Hodgkinson, 1985). Obviously, the first two groups will form a larger proportion of the general population (and especially the school population) in the future than is the case today. Table 4.2 shows the changes among these racial and ethnic groups that have taken place since 1980.

Table 4.2. Percent Change in U.S. Population by Race and Ethnicity, 1980 – 1990.

	Percent Increase
Total U.S.	9.8
White, non-Hispanic	6.0
Black	13.2
Native American, Eskimo, or Aleut	37.9
Asian or Pacific Islander	107.8
Hispanic (of any race)	53.0

Source: U.S. Bureau of the Census. Reproduced with permission of the Institute for Educational Leadership, Inc.

Because of the different cultural, socioeconomic, and educational characteristics of these groups, these changes will have a dramatic influence upon educational policy making. Although these percentages do not suggest that white, non-Hispanic Americans are becoming a national minority, they do point to some trends that affect local education agenda in very real ways. And when these changes are coupled with some of the other factors discussed below, their effect is greatly increased.

Uneven Distribution of Minorities and Youth

Even with data in hand on disparate racial and ethnic group growth rates, one cannot assume that these figures hold true across the nation, for there is a very uneven distribution of minorities among the fifty states. For example, in 1990, eleven states had nonwhite youth populations of 10 percent or less (Maine −2.8 percent and Vermont −2.4 percent). In addition, over the next twenty years, several other states will see only small increases in these populations (Pennsylvania will only grow from 16.1 percent nonwhite in 1990 to 18.7 percent in 2010, Ohio from 16.2 percent to 20.8 percent) (Hodgkinson, 1992).

And as the states become increasingly dissimilar in their racial and ethnic composition, the number of young people will become concentrated in fewer states (a reflection, in part, of the higher minority birth rates in those same states discussed above). By 2010, *more than half of the nation's 62.6 million children will be in nine states*: Texas, California, Florida, New York, Illinois, Georgia, Michigan, Ohio, and Pennsylvania. However, there is little consistency even among this group (e.g., the total number of youth will decline in Ohio and Pennsylvania, while California, Texas, and Florida will gain a whopping 1.8 million young persons) (Hodgkinson, 1992).

Regional Population Changes

During the 1980s, more than 90 percent of the nation's growth took place in the South and the West. Most amazing of all, three states (California, Texas, and Florida) accounted for half of that growth — the first time this has ever happened. Texas will become the second most populous state by the year 2000, dropping New York to third place. The bi-coastal nature of the growth patterns is also important (Georgia, North and South Carolina, and Virginia made relatively large gains, while the

Midwest and the mid-Atlantic region were the major losers) (Hodgkinson, 1992). Regional rates of growth of school populations have already begun to reflect these differences.

However, all this growth cannot be attributed to the rapid migration of the population to more hospitable climates. Instead, the ethnic birth rates mentioned above are responsible for most of the regional differences (e.g., increased birth rates in the Sun Belt are due mainly to minority births; conversely, Frost Belt declines are based primarily on fewer white population births) (Hodgkinson, 1985).

Aging of the Population

America as a whole, however, cannot continue to think of itself as a nation of brawny youth. Indeed, the average age of the total population is increasing perceptibly, and the schools will not escape the effects of this change. Nationwide, as Baby Boomers (those born immediately after World War II) grow older, the demand for adult, higher, and continuing education is increasing, while less pressure is being exerted on the elementary schools. "By 1992, half of all college students will be over 25 and 20 percent will be over 35" (Hodgkinson, 1985, 3).

Somewhat less obvious on the surface, but just as important in understanding the effects of cohort-aging on education, is the fact that in 1980, the average white was thirty-one years old, the average Black twenty-five, and the average Hispanic only twenty-two. In other words, as Black and Hispanic Americans move into peak child-bearing years, the average white is moving out. The results, in terms of evolving regional majority-minority patterns, are already being seen in California (where "minorities" make up a majority of the student population in its elementary schools), Texas (where more than 46 percent of its students are minorities), and America's largest cities (the twenty-five largest have student bodies made up primarily of "minorities") (Hodgkinson, 1985). And before the year 2010, more than half of the youth population in three states (California, Texas, and Florida) will be nonwhite (Hodgkinson, 1992).

Family Patterns

The traditional family (working father, housewife mother, and two or more school-age children living together) no longer stands as the norm in American society. From 1955, when that model represented 60 percent of U.S. households, a dramatic downward trend has resulted in only 6 percent of those same households reflecting a similar image in 1990. Of even more serious concern is the decrease in the percentage of *family* households (compared to all households), down from 74 percent in 1980 to 71 percent in 1990 (Hodgkinson, 1992). The changes of this type that occurred between 1980 and 1990 are shown in Table 4.3.

Most dramatic, and of most concern, is the number of children being born outside of marriage to teenage mothers. ''To be the third child of a child is to be very much 'at risk' in terms of one's future'' (Hodgkinson, 1985, 3) educationally and otherwise. Why? Children of teens tend to be born prematurely, which results in low birth weight, and low birth weight is a good predictor of learning difficulties when the child gets to school. Because of these factors, slightly more than 21 percent of the U.S.'s 3,300,000 annual births is almost guaranteed to be educationally retarded or ''difficult to teach'' (Hodgkinson, 1985).

In addition, the number of latchkey children, of whom there are at least four million in the U.S. today, is increasing. Their lives are very different from what Americans have historically expected to be the norm. For them, reality includes receiving whatever parental supervision they get by telephone, excessive hours spent watching TV and talking to friends on the phone, and generally fending for themselves. The problems, if any, that are generated by such a lifestyle are brought to school with them (Hodgkinson, 1985).

Table 4.3. Change in Household Type, U.S., 1980 – 1990.

	Number of Households, 1990	Percent Change
Total Households	93,347,000	+ 15.5
Married Couples, No Children*	27,780,000	+ 15.0
Married Couples, with Children*	24,537,000	– 1.7
Single Parent*		
—Women	6,599,000	+ 21.2
Single Parent*		
—Men	1,153,000	+ 87.2
Singles Living Alone	22,999,000	+ 25.7
Singles Living with Non-Relatives	4,258,000	+ 45.3

*Children under age 18.
Source: U.S. Bureau of the Census, Current Population Survey, *Household and Family Characteristics*.
Reproduced with permission of the Institute for Educational Leadership, Inc.

Poverty

In 1983, 14 million children comprised two-fifths of America's poor. Not surprisingly, these children were concentrated among the ethnic minorities, where childhood poverty rates reached 40 percent compared to 14 percent for nonminority children. Nor are the trends themselves very positive: from 1979 to 1983, the number of children in poverty grew by 3.7 million, increasing the percentage in poverty from 16 to 22 (Hodgkinson, 1985). This correlates positively with the large number of single-parent families who live in poverty, most of whom are Black or Hispanic. For example, in 1989, 54 percent of Black children and 33 percent of Hispanic children were living with a never-married mother (Hodgkinson, 1989). In fact, 90 percent of the increase in children born into poverty historically has come from these households (Hodgkinson, 1985).

PROJECTIONS

Based upon a comparison of the 1980 and 1990 census data, Hodgkinson (1992, 5 − 8) made the following projections:

1) The population of the U.S. will continue to grow, but at less than the 9.8 percent rate of the 1980 to 1990 period. After 2010, it will begin to stabilize, and immigration will become a major source of new citizens.

2) The nation's youth population (age 0 − 17) will increase by 4.6 percent between 1990 and 2000 but then *decrease* by 3.7 percent over the next ten years, resulting in a net gain of only .5 percent over the two decades. White youth numbers will decline by 3.8 percent over the period, while Blacks and Hispanics will continue to increase (+ 1.2 percent and + 2.6 percent respectively). The result will be an increase of more than 4.4 million nonwhite youth and a decrease of 3.8 million in the total number of white youth.

3) States will become increasingly dissimilar in terms of ethnic diversity during the next 20 years, with the nation's youth being concentrated in a smaller number of states (i.e., those states where the nonwhite percentage is largest). For example, more than half of the youth population in California, Texas, and Florida will be nonwhite before 2010.

Table 4.4. Percent Nonwhite Youth,*
Projections for 2010 for Selected States.

State	Percent Nonwhite	State	Percent Nonwhite
DC	93.2	Louisiana	50.3
Hawaii	79.5	Mississippi	49.9
Texas	56.9	New Jersey	45.7
California	56.9	Maryland	42.7
Florida	53.4	Illinois	41.7
New York	52.8	South Car.	40.1
U.S.	38.2		

*Age 0 – 17 years.
Source: U.S. Census Bureau, as cited in *American Demographics*, May 1989. Reproduced with permission of the Institute for Educational Leadership, Inc.

4) The increasing percentage of nonwhite youth by 2010 will create some interesting majority/minority situations (see Table 4.4).

5) Eighty-five percent of new workers in the year 2000 and beyond will be combinations of immigrants, women, and minorities.

6) As the total population increases but the youth population declines after 2010, the nation's average age will increase rapidly.

THE EDUCATIONAL CONSEQUENCES OF DEMOGRAPHIC CHANGE

In 1985, Hodgkinson predicted the following educational consequences of demographic change. With rare exception (noted below), little has changed since then to suggest that he was incorrect.

According to his predictions (1985, 10), American schools will experience:

1) An increase in children from poverty households

2) A similar increase in children from single-parent households

3) More children from minority backgrounds entering school

4) A smaller percentage of children who have had experiences in Head Start and similar programs, even though more will have been eligible

5) A larger number of children who were premature babies and therefore, more likely to experience learning difficulties

6) More children from homes where their parents are not married

7) More latchkey children and children from blended families as a result of remarriage of one original parent

8) More children from teenage mothers

9) Fewer white, middle class, suburban children, with day care (once the province of the poor) becoming a middle class norm as well, as more women enter the work force

10) A continuing decline in the level of retention of students to high school graduation in virtually all states, except for minorities, for whom the retention rates will increase

11) A continued drop in the number of minority high school graduates who apply for college

12) A continued decrease in the total number of high school graduates, with the decrease being concentrated most heavily in the Northeast

13) A continuing increase in the number of Black middle class students

14) Increasing numbers of Asian-American students, with more of these coming from Indonesia and other poorer countries, resulting in increasing language difficulties for many

15) A continuing high number of dropouts among Hispanic students, of whom only about 40 percent currently [1985] complete high school

16) Increasing numbers of talented minority youth choosing the military as their educational route, both due to cost and direct access to high technology [Hodgkinson, along with everyone else, did not anticipate the end of the Cold War and the subsequent reduction in the U.S. military.]

DEMOGRAPHIC CHANGE AT THE LOCAL LEVEL

It is within this rapidly changing demographic context that those who develop local tech prep initiatives must lay their plans. An understanding of this larger context will equip them to do their jobs better. However, they will also need to identify the local variations on these national themes. The key to success is to determine the differences, if any, between the national and local scenarios. Answering the following question will put local planners on the right track:

What is the effect of the changing demographic characteristics of my school, school district, and postsecondary institution and my community and service area upon our educational offerings?

Planners can then design a tech prep initiative that is consistent with both the national and local pictures, so that whether students leave the local community or stay, they will be well-served. To do so will require diligence on the planners' part, access to good information, and professional assistance in the analysis of the data, along with significant human and fiscal resources.

To skip this exercise, use inappropriate or out-of-date information or, in any way treat the demographic composition of a local tech prep target population lightly is to invite failure. Programs adopted or adapted from other areas where they may have been successful will wither and die, if they are transplanted in such unturned soil. The agricultural analogy is apt: *to be successful, one must dig deeply into the demographic complexities of the system in which they wish to plant tech prep.*

Putting Concepts into Practice: Collecting and Interpreting Local Demographic Data

Local tech prep practitioners may wish to use any or all of the following resources in collecting and interpreting local demographic data.

1) State data centers — Each state has one or more data centers from which pertinent demographic data and other information can be secured. For a list of these centers, including their addresses and telephone numbers, see Appendix A.

2) State departments of agriculture, tourism, economic development, human services, education, community colleges, and other such divisions of state government — These agencies often have data bases and other detailed sources of information that can be used in analyzing the local demographic contexts.

3) Local departments of health and social services — These local agencies also collect some of the information needed for planning appropriate educational initiatives, particularly that dealing with birth rates, childhood health and nutrition, premature births, and other indicators of later success or failure in school.

4) Cooperative extension services — Each state provides these services through their Land Grant University(ies). In addition to collecting, analyzing, storing, and disseminating information of the type needed for planning tech prep, cooperative extension specialists

(i.e., faculty members who are professional economists, sociologists, demographers, etc.) are available to assist in interpreting these data. Several state extension services also have extensive electronic data bases into which local educators may connect through the use of a telephone modem. Contact is made through your local cooperative extension office.

5) Departments of sociology, rural sociology, economics, political science, geography, etc. at local, regional, and state universities — Graduate students may be available to assist in data analysis and interpretation.

6) Local offices of major regional and national business and industrial firms — These organizations have extensive data bases that include information to which they may provide access. You may also secure assistance from their staff in analyzing and interpreting these demographic data and other pertinent information.

7) State banking associations and other business and trade associations — These organizations may be able to provide you with key data and information.

8) At last count, Hodgkinson had developed State Profiles for twenty-one states. Each of these profiles focuses on the cultural, demographic, and economic trends confronting state policy makers in those states. They may be ordered from The Institute for Educational Leadership, Publications Department, 1001 Connecticut Avenue N.W., Suite 310, Washington, DC 20036.

The Evolving Workplace

EDUCATORS AND THE WORKPLACE

THE point was made earlier that, as America enters the Information Age, the influence of the world's changing labor markets is being felt in every classroom. This would be true without the increasing competition from Japan and other countries for leadership in the international marketplace. With that competition serving as an additional goad behind many current cultural, political, and educational initiatives, the schools are being carried along on a current of change that many educators simply do not understand.

Only those who are well-informed about these changes will be able to maintain their integrity as educators while responding to the legitimate needs of potential employers of their students, whether those jobs be next door or halfway around the world. This requires generating and placing a second structural component into the conceptual foundation (see Figure 5.1).

By the very nature of their jobs, most educators are somewhat insulated from the realities of the world of work outside their classrooms. Nevertheless, understanding the evolving workplace is central to teachers restructuring their classrooms and administrators restructuring their schools in the ways that such a changing world demands. Questions to which answers must be found include:

What are the dynamics of change in the international, national, regional, and local labor markets? What competencies are needed for success in those changing labor markets? How do these competencies differ from those of yesterday and today?

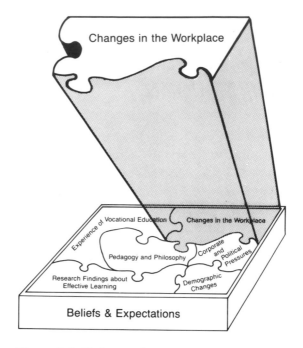

Figure 5.1 Understanding the evolving workplace.

WHAT'S REALLY GOING ON OUT THERE?

First of all, jobs are not where they used to be. Low-skilled jobs are disappearing, partly because of automation and partly because many are being moved to third world countries. Manufacturing will have a much smaller share of the American economy in the future. And there are those who say that between now and the turn of the century, service industries will create all of the new jobs and most of the new wealth in this country (NCEE, 1990).

In addition, the workforce itself is changing, growing older, more female, and more economically disadvantaged. The average age of today's worker is thirty-six. By the year 2000, it will be thirty-nine (NCEE, 1990). Shortly after the new millennium, 83 percent of the United States' new workers will be a combination of women, minorities, and immigrants (Hodgkinson, 1989). The implications are profound, particularly if a large percentage of these workers continues to be poorly served by schools, as is currently the case.

Perhaps, more importantly, the jobs that *do* exist are not the same as they once were. U.S. business was able to dominate the world's markets through most of the twentieth century because it invented and mastered the mass production factory model for producing goods. Key features of this model included minimal worker control, limited worker discretion, high levels of inventory, sophisticated quality control systems, and specialized personnel. This type of system is most advantageous when products and services, production systems, and technologies rarely change (Berryman and Bailey, 1992).

During that same period, true to its charge (which it has always taken from the private sector more than educators or corporate executives like to admit), the American school system turned out workers who fit these specifications *through schools built on that industrial model*. The problem is that the needs of the workplace can no longer be met by such a model, either in the plant or the schoolhouse.

That workplace is changing to an Information Age model (see Chart 5.1). Flexibility, fast response time, and innovation have joined cost as the keys to growth and competitiveness in today's international job market. Rather than a low-skilled, highly controlled system, the new economic environment requires the integration of traditionally separate roles (which alone has great implication for the restructuring of education), the flattening of organizational hierarchies, decentralization of responsibility, and greater employee involvement at all levels. This rapidly evolving system is more responsive, flexible, and conducive to continuous innovation, but it requires workers with different and, often, higher-level skills (Berryman and Bailey, 1992).

Conversely, it is also true that low-skill jobs—such as those in food service or simple clerical jobs—still exist in abundance and will continue to be the primary opportunities available to many first-time employees for some time to come. Moreover, few of these jobs can be restructured to require middle-level skills, and it is unreasonable to expect the small businesses in which most of these jobs exist to offer the training necessary for individuals to become upwardly mobile (Berryman, Knuth, and Law, 1992).

In addition, these entry-level jobs do not provide the wages or career paths necessary for young people to support and raise their families over the long term. Minimum wage, even in a two-income household, will barely pay the rent in today's economy. Little, if any, money is left for other needs such as adequate food, medical care, and transportation.

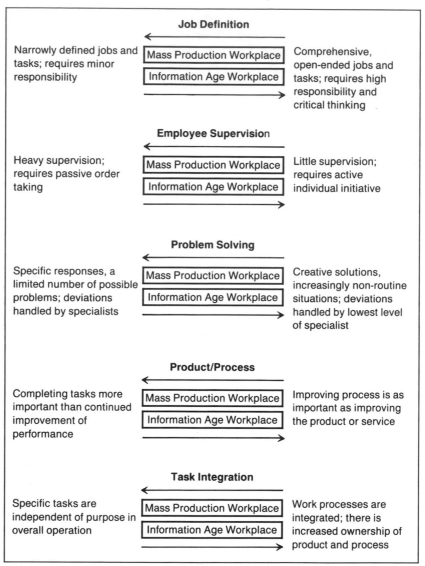

Chart 5.1 *Characteristics of traditional vs. future workplaces [adapted from Berryman, Knuth, and Law (1992)].*

Realizing the futility of remaining in these dead-end jobs, many workers become discouraged and resort to the welfare system. Increasingly, only middle-skill and higher-skill jobs pay wages that allow young people to begin and maintain a family (Berryman, Knuth, and Law, 1992).

COMPETENCIES NEEDED FOR SUCCESS
IN THE CHANGING LABOR MARKET

Such changes in the labor market result in major qualitative and quantitative shifts in competencies required for job success, both now and in the future. Economists argue that such shifts require workers with a much wider range of competency and skills than before, including a more abstract understanding of their tasks and how they relate to the entire production and marketing process of a firm. Group interaction and social skills will also become more important as the move to flexibility for both skilled and unskilled workers continues (Bailey, 1989). There may have been a time when the "three R's" were enough, but that time has passed, although they remain basic to successful employment.

These changes did not occur overnight. The handwriting has been on the wall for some time for those who were willing to read it, and the education establishment was given early notice. Almost thirty years ago, Lessinger warned that nothing in the high school program of that day prepared students properly for the increasingly diverse postsecondary opportunities and expectations. However, he was not without hope, nor did his hope rest on increasingly specialized instruction. Instead, he believed that ". . . underlying all the professional, skilled, and technical occupations (present and future) lies a substantial set of behaviors which can be taught, described, and are remarkably stable" (1965, 1).

In 1975, the author raised the concept of true "skill salability" with his fellow state directors of vocational education. Recognizing that a person's ability to adapt to a new job requiring new skills is an increasingly important measure of his/her usefulness to society, he argued that salability is a function of both the mastery of a specific skill for job entry and the transferability of that skill to other jobs for career stability. He further hypothesized that ". . . by the year 2000, we may see a reversal of the trend toward specialization. By then, the more theoretical the skill, the more salable it will be" (Law, 1975, 48–49).

Cetron and Gayle concluded that there is a growing mismatch between the literacy (vocabulary, reading, and writing skills) of the labor force and the competency required by the available and the soon-to-be-available jobs. The biggest mismatch will be among the best jobs, where educational demands are greatest. And, most disturbing of all, three-quarters of the new entrants into the job market will be qualified for only

40 percent of the new jobs created between 1985 and the year 2000 (1991, 222).

What is this new competency? Levin and Rumberger (1988) included the following as goals of formal education: *communication, reasoning, problem solving, obtaining and using information,* and *the ability to continue to learn.* They also listed the following "dispositions" as necessary for success in the workplace:

- the willingness to take the initiative and perform independently
- the ability to cooperate and work in groups
- competence in planning and evaluating one's own work and the work of others
- understanding how to work with persons from different backgrounds
- the ability to make decisions

In July 1991, the United States Secretary of Labor's Commission on Achieving Necessary Skills (SCANS) specified that after graduation from high school, all potential workers should possess the ability to:

- manage resources, such as money and time
- work as a team [member] and negotiate
- acquire and use information
- understand complex systems
- use technology

And possess:

- a solid foundation in basic skills, such as reading, writing, math, and speaking
- thinking skills, enabling them to detect and to solve problems
- high personal qualities, enabling them to work well with others (see Charts 5.2 and 5.3)

Workers of the future will need to operate more independently in a less well-defined environment, which requires a greater facility for creative thinking, decision making, reasoning, and problem solving. They will also need a broader understanding of the systems in which they operate, so they can monitor and correct the performance of those systems and participate in the improvement of their design. But, most of all, they will need a more abstract or conceptual understanding of what they are doing. This understanding will allow them to carry out tasks and solve problems that they have neither performed before nor been shown specifically how to carry out or solve. Thus, more than in the

1. Basic Skills	2. Thinking Skills	3. Personal Qualities
Reading: Locates, understands, and interprets written information in prose and in documents such as manuals, graphs, and schedules	**Creative Thinking:** Generates new ideas	**Responsibility:** Exerts a high level of effort and perseveres toward goal attainment
Writing: Communicates thoughts, ideas, information, and messages in writing; creates documents such as letters, directions, manuals, reports, graphs, and flow charts	**Decision Making:** Specifies goals and constraints, considers risks, and evaluates and chooses the best alternative	**Self-Esteem:** Believes in own self-worth and maintains a positive view of self
	Problem Solving: Recognizes problems and devises and implements plan of action	**Sociability:** Demonstrates understanding, friendliness, adaptability, empathy, and politeness in group settings
Arithmetic and Math: Performs basic computations and approaches practical problems by choosing appropriately for a variety of math techniques	**Visualizing:** Organizes and processes symbols, pictures, graphs, objects, and other information	**Self-Management:** Assesses self accurately, sets personal goals, monitors progress, and exhibits self-control
Listening: Receives, attends to, interprets, and responds to verbal messages and other cues	**Knowing How to Learn:** Uses efficient learning techniques to acquire and apply new knowledge and skills	**Integrity/Honesty:** Chooses ethical courses of action
Speaking: Organizes ideas and communicates orally	**Reasoning:** Discovers a rule or principle underlying the relationship between two or more objectives and applies it when solving a problem	

Chart 5.2 SCANS foundation (tool) skills [adapted from Berryman, Knuth, and Law (1992)].

past, individuals will need to be able to acquire, organize, and interpret information for themselves (Berryman and Bailey, 1992).

Raizen (1991) characterized two different types of futures for American workers: the better educated can expect expanding opportunities and rising wages, the poorly educated face a future of poverty and contracting opportunities. For students, the choice is clear. They can either invest in the education that lets them weather the coming changes in the labor market, or they can slip into the unrewarding realm of the permanent underclass.

1.	Identifies, organizes, plans, and allocates resources including time, money, material, facilities, and human resources
2.	Works with others (interpersonal skills) by participating as a member of a team, teaching others new skills, serving clients as customers, exercising leadership, negotiating, and working in a heterogeneous workplace
3.	Acquires and uses information, including skills of evaluation, organization, maintenance, interpretation, communication, and computer use
4.	Understands complex social, organizational, and technological inter-relationships (systems) and works and operates effectively with them, improves or designs them, and monitors and corrects performance
5.	Works with a variety of technologies, including their selection, application to tasks, and maintenance and troubleshooting

Chart 5.3 *SCANS generic workplace skills [adapted from Berryman, Knuth, and Law (1992)].*

Success, then, in the educational and economic marketplace of today and the future requires:

- basic literacy skills (i.e., reading, writing, computing, and thinking)
- the desire and ability to learn from every situation
- human relations skills
- information management skills
- specific job skills sufficient to gain entry into some recognized career or onto some type of occupational ladder
- an in-depth understanding of theory and concepts that allows individuals to transfer and apply all the above to meet the challenges and respond to the opportunities that will confront them as they identify and begin to move up their own career ladder

The latter understanding appears to be that which is needed most and about which the least is known, both in terms of how it works and how to help students acquire it.

CHARACTERISTICS OF EVOLVING LOCAL LABOR MARKETS

The conditions identified above create an umbrella of change under which local tech prep initiatives operate. However, practitioners must be most concerned with the marketplaces in which their students find entry level employment. And most students, secondary and postsecondary alike, find their first jobs locally, bringing to center court the following questions for the tech prep practitioner:

What are the dynamics of change in the local labor market? What competencies are needed for success in this labor market? How do these competencies differ from those of yesterday and today? Is my local instructional program teaching these competencies? If not, what changes must we make?

Putting Concepts into Practice: Meshing Instructional Programs with Local Labor Market Needs

Most practitioners are familiar with the traditional ways of determining the needs of the local labor market. But important as they are, employer surveys and the data provided by the local Employment Security Commission office only go so far. Those who wish to have a better grasp of the situation and answer the above questions more fully, may wish to try some or all of the following activities:

1) Identify the job cluster upon which you will focus by analyzing the labor market with the assistance of employers. Pay equal attention to needs and interests of students.

2) Get representatives from that career cluster to identify the competencies (academic, vocational, and technical) necessary for successful entry into and promotion in that cluster. If a postsecondary curriculum DACUM (Developing a Curriculum) process has been implemented and/or a secondary competency-based curriculum has been developed (e.g., V-TECS, NOCTI, or MECC) for courses within the cluster, start with, articulate, and build upon these materials.

3) If neither a DACUM nor a secondary competency-based curriculum exists, identify the tasks in that cluster in which employees are expected to be proficient. Break these down into specific competencies (academic and technical) using a valid and reliable process (e.g., DACUM or similar approach). Get help from your state education department staff on this task.

4) Place these competencies into a continuum that leads from the more simple to the most complex.

5) Review all the curricular components of your tech prep course of study to identify where these competencies can be taught best and any gaps or duplications that may exist.

6) Organize your program of study so that students are assured of achieving the requisite competencies before they leave you. Develop a curriculum matrix that specifies the courses to be taken, in sequence, to obtain the competencies.

7) Identify and agree upon the evaluation process and instruments that will be used throughout the system (secondary and postsecondary) to evaluate the competency level reached by students as they move through the program of study.

8) Secure short-term employment or internships for selected teachers in jobs for which students are being prepared to give them experience in the required competencies.

Corporate and Political Influence

NO other single feature dominated the political landscape of the 1980s like the sudden surge of interest shown by corporate leaders of American business and industry in improving education. Historically, such interest has translated into a political agenda, and this time was no exception. Whatever educators may think or feel about this phenomenon, they cannot escape it.

The concerns expressed by corporate-political coalitions are real to them, and practitioners must learn to fit them into the educational scheme of things *without* abdicating their educational responsibilities. To deal with them most appropriately requires understanding the place of this factor in the conceptual foundation and its interaction with the other components that comprise that foundation (see Figure 6.1).

Practitioners can begin to come to grips with this perplexing dilemma, through answers to the following questions:

What corporate and political pressures are influencing American education? How do these pressures interact? What is the result of these pressures on national and state views about tech prep?

TUNING IN TO THE MESSAGE

John L. Clendenin, chairman and chief executive officer of BellSouth Corporation, stated the position of American business on education quite succinctly as he took over the reins of the U.S. Chamber of Commerce: "No business can afford not to be terribly concerned about the education crisis facing the United States today. It bears directly on our *competitiveness* [emphasis added] as a nation" (Gray, 1989, 61).

And although the more than 200 business leaders, politicians, and educators who came to *Fortune* magazine's "Summit II" in 1989 agreed

73

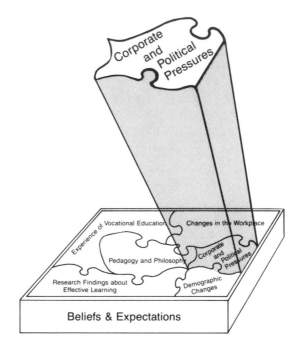

Figure 6.1 *Corporate and political influences.*

that business can't brandish any kind of big stick, they also agreed that corporations can do plenty to *push* education in a different direction. Said Apple Computer's John Sculley: "Chief executives of global enterprises are becoming as powerful as many heads of state" (Perry, 1989, 138). So it is hardly surprising that the conferees concluded: "America must expect more of its schools, its children, and itself in order to compete in a global marketplace where mental *might* is increasingly the quality that separates *winners* from *losers* [emphasis added]" (Perry, 1989, 137).

Although they acknowledge that the world is moving toward a global economy, it is somewhat ironic that the rhetoric of corporate and political leaders on the subject of education is competitive (see above) and, at times, combative. And in the same vein, as solutions have been posed, more punitive action against the purported guilty parties (i.e., the educational bureaucracy and educators in general) has been condoned and even recommended. "*Threat* [emphasis added] is helpful," concluded Governor Thomas Kean of New Jersey (Perry, 1989, 138).

Berryman and Bailey (1992) question the appropriateness of such aggressive rhetoric, specifically taking issue with the assumption of a causal link between improved skills of individual students and national economic competitiveness. However, for many in the corporate community, this assumption appears to be quite logical, since they believe the problem to be pretty simple, for example:

> Isn't education basically a simple matter after all? I mean, great books, some mathematics, great teachers, discipline, and time. That's about it, with a little computer literacy thrown in for modern measure. (Weimer, 1992, 84)

There are businesspeople who reach different conclusions. Nan Stone, managing editor of the *Harvard Business Review*, said, ''. . . it is not the performance level of students that has declined. Rather, the demands of the external competitive environment have increased'' (1991, 47). Hers is apparently a minority position, however, for most in the private sector seem to share perceptions similar to Weimer's.

Nor have they been timid about saying so. Writing for *Forbes* in March, 1992, William Tucker noted that ''public education is a $230-billion-a-year industry that badly needs the discipline of a market system to make it responsive to its customers'' (1992, 88). At an earlier time, he had identified what he believed to be the problem by quoting John Chubb, a senior fellow at the Brookings Institution and co-author of *Politics, Markets & America's Schools:* ''. . . the current bureaucratic system does everything it can to take that autonomy [necessary for success] away from individual schools'' (1991, 180).

The logic of the corporate world (a trifle overstated here, but not too far off the mark) seems to be: America is faced with a sagging economy and is no longer competitive in the markets of the world because our workers lack the requisite technical skills. Our public schools, which get an inordinate amount of our tax dollars, should have been teaching these skills all along. And they would have, if it had not been for the ''bureaucracy.'' Let's remove the bureaucrats and run schools more like businesses. If it works for business, it should do just fine for education.

It matters not that the bureaucratic structure of schools is a replica of successful business organizations of the past seventy-five years (admittedly now out of date), or that most business enterprises have only recently begun to restructure themselves. In fact, Berryman and Bailey (1992) worry about the need for workplace restructuring *before* employers will be ready to accept students from a restructured school. And although it is true that the strategies advocated by Deming (1986) have begun to be implemented in many businesses, the private sector has much to do to get its own house in order. Witness, for example, the "bottom-line," short-term thinking that still exists in many companies, the "take-over" mentality that dominated the 1980s, the reluctance of many corporations to reorganize their work, and the most recent tendency to "downsize" the production of almost everything from crackers to computers, while emphasizing the importance of technology over people.

This is not to suggest that schools do not need to change. Indeed, they must. Nor does it suggest any reluctance to adopt Deming's principles for meeting consumer demand. Rather, it is to suggest that blind obeisance by educators to what appear to be the laws of commerce and business will, in the long run, be more harmful than helpful to all concerned.

CORPORATE-POLITICAL AFFINITIES

All this notwithstanding, the political world is keenly attuned to these corporate vibrations, and politicians have been quick to note the importance of the education reform movement, particularly when it seems to embody the wishes and needs of the corporate power structure. They flock to such potential power bases at the first opportunity (e.g., many became more than willing participants in the 1980s phenomenon known as the "education summit").

Whatever their value may have been, anyone conversant with recent events is aware of the number of these summits that have been held in the past few years. President George Bush's calling of the governors to Charlottesville, Virginia, in September, 1989, is probably the preeminent example. But the corporate world has not been far behind. A good example is *Fortune* magazine's earlier-mentioned "Summit II."

A close look at the participants in that particular meeting gives one a peek at the powerful coalitions being forged between the corporate and political sectors of American society in the name of education. In attendance were Governors Terry E. Branstad, Iowa; Rudy Perpich, Minnesota; Thomas H. Kean, New Jersey; and Roy Romer, Colorado. CEOs attending included William A. Schreyer, Merrill Lynch; John Sculley, Apple Computer; Jerre L. Stead, Square D; and David T. Kearns, Xerox

(Perry, 1989). And this gathering was by no means exceptional in this regard.

Further evidence of these alliances is found in the membership of the "Blue Ribbon" commissions that have been appointed at the national and state levels since the publishing of *A Nation at Risk*. The nation has also witnessed the spawning of a multitude of "education governors" and even an "education president." And there are the increasingly powerful business/political/educational organizations exerting major influence upon state educational policy making (e.g., the North Carolina and Mississippi Public School Forums).

While the corporate sector cannot, in and of itself, mandate a particular brand of educational reform, the political leaders who are their partners in such coalitions can and do. Most readers will remember former-Secretary of Education William Bennett's use of the Federal government's "bully pulpit." The message became even more pointedly business-oriented when Lamar Alexander, former governor of Tennessee, was appointed to that same position, and he, in turn, tapped David Kearns of Xerox to join him as deputy secretary.

Upon being asked if, when he was governor, he got much business cooperation in his Better Schools program, Alexander replied, "What I needed in terms of cooperation at the beginning was in breaking down the barriers" (Baker, 1989, 24). And after coming to his new position in the Department of Education, Kearns commented, ". . . if there isn't some pressure on the system, I know that it won't change. I think business can bring [that] pressure" (Szabo, 1991, 25).

Voices from the Past

This passion for education on the part of corporate leaders is nothing new, although it does wax and wane with the state of the economy. At the turn of the century, American industrialists were faced with a similar need for more highly skilled employees. They had previously depended primarily upon unskilled labor, but were now forced into relying increasingly upon apprenticeship programs (a situation they felt to be intolerable). In its place, the industrialists wanted ". . . practical trade training" (Cremin, 1961, 33).

Not surprisingly, international competition also played a role. At that time, Germany dominated world markets, and Germany had a system of successful trade schools. America seemed to have everything necessary for success except those same trade schools. Then, as now, business and industry turned to (and, at times, upon) the schools. Their podium became the newly organized (1895) National Association of Manufacturers (NAM). In 1905, the NAM's Committee on Industrial Education issued its first report, which cited figures on the school dropout problem, criticized the schools for failing to meet the needs of most students, called most school programs impractical and boring, and proposed trade schools as the logical answer.

Playing to a Mixed Review

However, just as there was suspicion of the motives behind corporate involvement in education at the turn of the century (Wirth, 1972), a similar skepticism still exists. Emerson Schiller, a Chicago educator, argues that educational reform may, like beauty, be in the eye of the beholder. After characterizing the interest of big business in education as one of limiting the intellectual options for workers' children and reducing education to a job-related minimum, he shares his concern that some of today's corporate reform schemes seem to ". . . call for upgrading of schools for the few, but contain hidden mechanisms by which education for the many will be sharply set back in quality" (Schiller, 1989, 10).

On the other hand, there are educators who believe that *far too little* has been done, and that corporate leadership has been *much too easy* on the educational establishment. Chester E. Finn, Jr., a former assistant secretary of education, complains, "Throughout the United States, the most conspicuous feature of business involvement with the schools has been soft-headedness" (1989, 34). Back on the opposite end of the spectrum, ". . . a national moratorium on reforms, so that educators and local policy makers can analyze their own problems," would please others (Orlich, 1989, 517).

Calling for a more balanced approach, Hoyt (1991) argues that there is confusion and a lack of clarity about the respective roles of the private sector and education in educational reform. He recommends that educators and private sector persons share responsibility and authority for helping students *and* that ". . . they must also share accountability for the success of those students" (1991, 451). For educators to share responsibility and authority with corporate partners is a reasonable suggestion with which most persons, educators and corporate representatives alike, are likely to agree. To suggest that comparable *account-ability* should be expected of both parties plows new ground and needs to be incorporated into future dialogue on the topic.

Suggesting that business may live in a glass house and should, therefore, not be prone to throw too many rocks, Stone acknowledges that ". . . business often sees the schools' problems far more clearly than it sees its own" (Stone, 1991, 46). She suggests that by attending to the educational and training needs of their current employees, corporate America can make major improvements in its competitive stance in the international marketplace, while setting a much better example for schools.

Perhaps the wave of the future will include the simultaneous restructuring of both the workplace and the schools, using the best minds of both the corporate sector and education. Those in both quarters who promote the use of TQM place a great deal of hope in this possibility.

There Is Sufficient Fault to Go Around

If the corporate sector has been portrayed here as somewhat heavy-handed in their relationship with the schools, the fault is by no means all theirs. "There is nothing new about calling for connections between the private sector and the education system" (Hoyt, 1991, 450), but educators have seldom been comfortable in the ensuing relationships. Nor have they seemed to know how to cooperate or collaborate in such efforts, much less take the initiative. Typically, their reaction has been one of either manning the battlements or resignedly abdicating their responsibilities. Neither response evokes a very positive image with those in the corporate world who are truly trying to help. Nor does either strategy help those most in need—the students.

Yet, almost invariably, when asked what kind of assistance is needed to educate students better, the field has answered: more money. Doubtless, education is not funded sufficiently, but to have a single response held at-the-ready for all questions or criticisms that come one's way is self-defeating.

The resources that the corporate world can bring to a partnership are almost beyond the comprehension of most educators. To access these resources, educators must:

1) Take the initiative and exert leadership in education reform.
2) Refrain from being defensive about everything (save the energy for the truly important issues).
3) Admit education has some real problems and identify them.
4) Work with corporate citizens to review these problems and identify possible responses that the private sector might help educators make.
5) Develop a plan for jointly addressing the problems and evaluating the results.

GUIDELINES FOR WORKING TOGETHER

For educators to work effectively with the private sector, they need an objective and balanced perspective. Such a view will recognize that:

1) America's economy is truly suffering, and this affects everyone.
2) At least part of the reason for this relatively weak economy is the lack of competitiveness of American workers, especially in fields of high technology.
3) The workplace is changing dramatically and will require more workers who are conceptually well-grounded (particularly in mathematics, communication, and science), technically competent, and most importantly, motivated and know how to learn.
4) America's schools are not currently organized to provide these kinds of intellectual and technical skills to a large majority of their students.
5) The artificial differences between work and learning are disappearing. The effectively restructured workplace and the appropriately restructured school will look a lot alike.
6) The corporate world has a strong and positive vested interest in improving education and has a great deal it can contribute to that process.
7) However, the answer is not one of restructuring schools to mimic the current state of affairs in the largest (or smallest) corporations. Nor is it found in the potential largesse of these corporations in funding additional education programs.
8) It lies, instead, in educators and corporate representatives cooperatively identifying and then sharing in the solving of real problems in education *and* the workplace.

Working together, creative educators and corporate representatives may uncover veritable gold mines in each others' backyards, *if* they begin the process as equals committed to the same values, goals, and ideals. To their surprise, corporate citizens may find some of the solutions to their own structural problems in the school setting.

This is not a simple or a short-term process. At a minimum, it will take organization, *time* to get to know one another, creative analysis and problem solving, *time* to build up trust, identification and sharing of resources, *time* to learn how to work cooperatively and collaboratively, experimental thought and planning processes, *time* to try the proposed solutions, exacting documentation and evaluation techniques, and *time* to modify and improve the process.

POLITICAL AND CORPORATE PRESSURES AT THE LOCAL LEVEL

Many of the criticisms reported above are also heard at the local school, school district, and postsecondary institution level. Part of this is due to the national character of many of the businesses and industrial organizations that employ locally. Part comes from the networks that exist among business and industrial leaders and part from what they read and hear through their national and state trade associations.

The pressure that the corporate and political world can bring to bear upon local practitioners is powerful and can be difficult to withstand—if viewed as a threat. Pure defensiveness on the part of the educator is sure to fail. Passive acquiescence is of no more value in the long run. The question becomes one of how to deal with these pressures professionally.

Astute educators will do well to analyze these national, state, and local pressures, whatever their sources, and build upon those that are positive and consistent with local educational goals and objectives. To do so, they need to answer the following questions:

What corporate and political pressures are influencing education at the local level? How do these pressures interact? What is the result of these pressures on the local view of tech prep? How can I use these pressures to effect long-term and positive educational change in my school, school district, and postsecondary institution?

Local practitioners must be sensitive not only to what is being said by corporate leaders and politicians, but to what their words may actually mean. In spite of the somewhat confrontational words and antagonistic tones taken at times, it is highly unlikely that these persons are nearly as confident in their proposed solutions as they may seem. Nor are they enemies of education and educators. The dilemma lies in their not knowing better ways of approaching what, to them, is a very real and frustrating problem (i.e., students who don't seem to learn well who end up on their doorsteps as technically illiterate would-be workers). Most corporate citizens have more questions than answers and will gladly relinquish the initiative and leadership for reforming education to any educator who is willing to tackle what they view as real problems.

Putting Concepts into Practice: Connecting with the Corporate and Political Sectors

To be successful during the next decade, school and school system leaders must learn how to connect with the corporate and political sectors of their community. Meaningful partnerships can be established. The most effective partnerships will be those in which open-minded educators take the first step. The following suggestions are provided for those who wish to move in that direction:

1) Take the initiative. Don't wait for local corporate or political leaders to come to you (or worse, go to the press) with their concerns about education.

2) Develop a long-range comprehensive plan for reforming and restructuring education (K − 14) in your community and service area. Involve corporate and political leadership in the planning process from the outset. If such a plan already exists, modify it, if necessary, to incorporate the legitimate concerns of the corporate community.

3) Request assistance from your corporate community in developing this plan. Ask for their experts in long-range planning, demographics, and labor market statistics. Request permission to access their electronic data bases for information you may need.

4) Ask your local chambers of commerce for any formal positions they may have taken on and recommendations they may have made about education. Ask them to appoint a committee to work with you to identify problems and design solutions.

5) Take the plan to key corporate and political leaders for their input at critical points in its development, and *use the input you get.*

6) Once the goals and objectives are set, publicize them as thoroughly and as often as possible in the corporate and political communities.

7) Form a committee comprised of educators and corporate representatives to identify contributions the corporate community can make toward meeting the stated goals and objectives of the plan for change.

8) Survey your corporate community to identify any organizations that are currently undergoing restructuring of their own, particularly those training their staff in and adopting the principles of total quality management. If possible, enter into a partnership with these organizations to share the restructuring experience.

9) Remember that such an approach is most likely to succeed when it has a specific purpose and focus, a limited set of goals and objectives, and a well-trained staff comprised of educators and corporate representatives who are totally committed to the long-term improvement of systemic quality.

10) Above all else, recognize that the long-term systemic changes you seek will not come in a day, a month, or even a year, no matter which and how many of your biggest corporations are helping you. Take it one day at a time, and get everyone involved for the "long haul." You'll be surprised at how much the corporate sector can help you accomplish when *you* learn how best to help them contribute. And you'll learn the skills you need to master only by trying it out. To paraphrase John Dewey, you'll just have to learn to do it by doing it.

Recent Research into Effective Instruction

UNDERSTANDING the changing demographics of America, as well as its evolving workplace, and identifying the competencies needed for success in that workplace are essential steps in building an effective tech prep initiative. The question now becomes one of designing and implementing instructional strategies that help students develop those proficiencies. This brings practitioners face to face with the following question, through which yet another component of the conceptual foundation is laid in place (see Figure 7.1):

What does the latest research teach about the process of effective teaching and learning?

HOW DO PEOPLE REALLY LEARN BEST?

While the schools reeled from the attacks mounted following the release of *A Nation at Risk*, cognitive scientists have been hard at work developing a clearer understanding of just how people really do learn. And many time-honored beliefs of education are fast approaching myth-like status, such as the presumption that students must acquire a specific set of basic skills before further education can take place. Although debates have historically been carried on about exactly what these basic skills are or should be, there has always been general agreement among educators that there is a core of knowledge and skills that must be mastered as a foundation for all other learning (Raizen, 1989).

However, recent research raises serious questions about this premise of "first things first," the evidence suggesting instead that many people do not learn in logical, linear patterns. For most, it is much more complex and far more likely to be a holistic experience, rather than a series of singular acts.

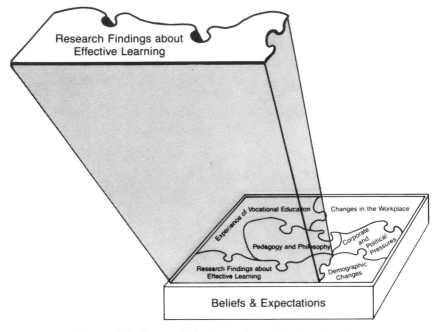

Figure 7.1 *Research findings about effective learning.*

For example, what is now known about how individuals learn and use basic mathematical and reading skills is creating doubts about even these most commonly accepted skill hierarchies. Many people seem to be able to acquire mathematical skills and generate their own efficient procedures for solving arithmetic problems in the work context or in real life outside work, but, in a paradoxical turn of events, cannot solve similar problems in a formal school setting (Raizen, 1989). Nor are such learning patterns restricted to lower-level skills: "... thinking sustained by daily human sense can be — in the same subject — at a higher level than thinking out of context" (Donaldson, 1978, 27).

The typical teaching of mathematics in formal school settings tends to overlook the importance of meaning, which lowers students' performance (Carraher, 1986). The same holds true for reading and science (e.g., marginally literate adults made twice the gain in job-related reading than they did in general reading) (Sticht, 1987). In other words, they did better when a meaningful context was provided. In science, researchers have learned that even very young children bring their own experiential knowledge (correct and incorrect) about the workings of the world in which they live to the classroom (Raizen, 1989).

In fact, every person brings a personally meaningful knowledge base to each new learning experience, where they then use it to organize their perceptions and increase their grasp of the world about them. Right or wrong, these perceptions are their starting point. If properly approached, teachers can identify and begin with this base of knowledge, modify it if necessary, and help the learners increase their perceptual knowledge and therefore, their capacity to make sense of their world (Caine and Caine, 1991).

But Schools Aren't Organized That Way

But most school subjects are not organized to facilitate the students' use of their own knowledge bases. For example, as the former executive director of the National Science Teachers Association acknowledges, most science courses are highly abstract and theoretical and do not use appropriate pedagogical practices. He argues that science should be taught from the concrete (with which students are familiar) to the abstract, using examples that apply its principles to what students perceive to be practical and real. Beyond learning scientific facts, students taught in such fashion ". . . will know how and when to ask questions, how to think critically, and be able to make important decisions based on reason rather than on emotion or superstitions" (Aldridge, 1989). It should come as no surprise that these are the very skills being demanded at all levels in the changing world of work.

Somewhere along the way, however, educators seem to have picked up the mistaken notion that content can be taught apart from context, particularly the context of the workplace, and that ". . . what happens in the classroom is unaffected by the real world children and adults inhabit" (Caine and Caine, 1991). In reality, what people know through their experience exerts a very powerful influence upon what they learn in the classroom (Raizen, 1989). And when schools fail to acknowledge this ability of students to learn from experience, they fail the students (Caine and Caine, 1991).

What cognitive, anthropological, and brain research is also telling educators is that people learn through experience and on the job in ways that are decidedly *different* from the formal process enforced in most school settings. In addition, outside of school, they *use* what they already know and what they subsequently learn differently. These findings should not be particularly surprising, if one remembers any of the teachings of John Dewey. Yet historically, schools have neither taken these differences into account nor granted legitimacy to learning that occurs beyond their formal boundaries or realms of influence.

In fact, only recently has much attention been paid to the inconsistencies of school-based instruction and learning in the real world. For example, Resnick (1987, 16) created quite a stir when she identified four major discontinuities between education as practiced in school and the way people are expected to learn in daily life and work:

1) Schools focus on individual performance as contrasted to socially shared performance in most non-school settings.
2) The school model emphasizes unaided thought, whereas work makes available and even requires the use of cognitive tools.
3) Schools emphasize symbolic thinking to the exclusion of the objects and situations that aid formulation and solution in real life and at work.
4) Schools attempt to inculcate general skills and knowledge, rather than the situation-linked knowledge and skills that make for effective performance outside school.

These inconsistencies did not come about by accident. For years, teachers have intentionally presented learning opportunities devoid of context to students to enable them to acquire general skills, because they have believed this was the most effective way to teach. The underlying assumption, incorrect though it may be, has been that students will transfer these skills to a variety of other learning and work situations.

Unfortunately, the instruction that follows this assumption all too often takes place through isolated sub-tasks in which the emphasis is upon satisfactory repetitive performance of the sub-task, rather than on the use of the skill or information embedded in the sub-task in relevant contexts (Raizen, 1989). Evidence is mounting that such a fractured approach is self-defeating, not even achieving the in-school learning goals for which it was created (Resnick, 1987). Not only are students who are taught this way unable to transfer what they are supposed to learn to the outside world, they are not even successful in transferring it to other school-based learning experiences. This is not particularly surprising, for Caine and Caine (1991) argue that such an educational approach, which seldom goes beyond memorization of facts and specific skills, ignores much of the capacity of a person's brain.

It is important to note here that formal schooling is not context-free. However, the context in which it takes place seldom models any work situation learners are likely to confront. This is true even for future teachers, if current reform efforts achieve their anticipated results in the classroom.

On the other hand, secondary schools do typically emulate their faculty members' perceptions of the higher education context that they experienced. In such a setting, college preparatory students are given yet another advantage. Such is the insidious nature of the cultural bias towards the baccalaureate experience and against the work experience in American culture and, thus, in its schools.

In the one case in which the school setting does seem to depict an actual job setting fairly accurately, it may contribute to the relative success of that particular instructional program. Business education curricula experience a measure of success, probably because the school presents a contextual pattern similar to the kinds of structures in which many clerical and secretarial personnel have worked in the past—hierarchical and bureaucratized (Raizen, 1989). However, this too is likely to change as the workplace evolves.

Is There a Better Way?

According to the latest research on how the brain actually works, *multiple complex and concrete experiences are essential for meaningful learning to take place.* Students learn from their entire experience, and the reality for most of them is that content and context are virtually inseparable. The larger patterns of their existence can and need to be grasped by the learner, for ". . . the part is always embedded in a whole, the fact in multiple contexts, and a subject is always related to many other issues and subjects'' (Caine and Caine, 1991, 4).

Effective instruction, therefore, empowers students to access the knowledge they bring with them to the classroom to build new knowledge. And once again, it should be noted that the effectiveness of this approach is not limited to the better students. For example, remedial instruction is especially improved when teachers integrate specific knowledge and skills with reading, writing, arithmetic, and problem solving. Finally, when learning contexts (including tasks, materials, and procedures) are used that mirror real work tasks and situations as closely as possible, students can be clear about what they are to learn and why, as well as how the knowledge and skills they are acquiring can be applied in their own lives (Resnick, 1987).

It is not being suggested here that theory and abstractions should not be presented to students. Indeed, the opposite is true. It is being suggested that *students are more likely to understand the underlying theories and abstractions — which they desperately need in order to be successful after the secondary and postsecondary education experience — when their meaning is explored in detail within the context of specific situations with which they are familiar* (Raizen, 1989).

LEARNING FROM AN ANCIENT EXAMPLE

Apprenticeship is one of the world's oldest forms of education and centers on the practice of immersing students in the culture of the workplace they wish to join. Over the centuries, apprenticeship has proven effective in many situations. Although it is neither possible nor appropriate to completely restructure American public education on the apprenticeship model, there are lessons to be learned from it that can be applied to formal schooling. For example, recent studies (Jordan, 1989) point out that:

1) Apprenticeship happens as a way of life, with almost no separation between daily activities and the learning of professional skills.
2) Activities are organized around the work that must be accomplished, with mastery appreciated for its immediate use and value, rather than as a step toward a certificate or the next level of learning.
3) The order of skill learning tends to be from the periphery to the central activity, but it does not proceed in linear, chronologically ordered sequences predetermined by others.
4) Performance lies in doing something, rather than talking about it.
5) Evaluation of the learner's competence is implicit, rather than explicit, effective performance being obvious to both master and apprentice.

SUMMARY

Most people seem to learn best when:

1) That which they already know is recognized, respected, and built upon.

2) The information and skills to be learned are presented as part of a natural environment in which they make sense and are of immediate utility (or as nearly so as possible) to the learner.

3) The learning environment is as tension-free as possible.

4) The teacher and learners interact freely and regularly with their environment and one another.

5) The learning experience proceeds from the specific to the general and from the practical to the theoretical.

6) The learner is given immediate feedback.

7) The learning experience encourages different and creative learning styles on the part of the learner.

PUTTING CONCEPTS INTO PRACTICE: IDENTIFYING AND CONNECTING WITH OTHER EDUCATIONAL REFORM INITIATIVES

As stated earlier, those who lead tech prep all too often do not look at the larger educational reform movement and its research base for assistance. Through their short-sightedness, they not only guarantee the continued isolation of tech prep, they also risk being left far behind in terms of effective instructional innovation. For those local practitioners who wish to identify, connect with, and build upon these other initiatives, the following questions are appropriate:

How can the latest findings about the process of effective teaching and learning be built into a local tech prep initiative? What other instructional reform initiatives are taking place in my school, school district, and postsecondary institution? Upon what pedagogical (teaching/learning) premises are they built? What are the pedagogical connections between these activities and our vision of tech prep?

The following activities may facilitate finding answers to these questions:

1) Form a partnership with the district-level staff who are responsible for curriculum and instruction. Find out what innovative instructional initiatives are under way in the district and elsewhere.

2) Contact local, state, and national offices of curriculum and instruction professional organizations, such as the Association for Supervision and Curriculum Development (ASCD).

3) Pay special attention to early childhood and middle school initiatives.

4) Check with local and state mathematics leadership to see if any of the recommendations of the National Council of Teachers of Mathematics (NCTM) are being implemented in the district or in nearby schools in other districts.

5) Look for "whole language" and "writing across the curriculum" programs.

6) Determine what, if any, innovation is taking place in your science course offerings.

7) Look for any programs using principles of brain-based learning, cooperative learning, outcome-based education, team teaching, and integration of instruction.

8) Identify those teachers and others who are the most effective implementers of innovative activities. Help them work through their philosophies and pedagogical strategies and synthesize them into a common approach to improving instruction.

9) Conduct staff development for all teachers, using the identified teachers as teacher-trainers, gradually moving the entire instructional program toward a more context-specific and experientially based approach.

CONCLUSIONS

Raizen (1989, 59) ended her work by suggesting that what needs to be done in American education seems "simple enough":

1) Integrate learning of basic skills with learning about the devices, systems, procedures, decision rules, and social interactions characteristic of specific work settings and responsibilities.

2) Provide most education for work in settings that are, or duplicate

as closely as possible, the work setting for which the individual is preparing, while ensuring that the necessary guidance and tutoring are provided.

3) Ensure that the education being provided is not narrowly limited in its scope.

4) Take into account the personal lives of the student or novice worker and recognize the interrelationships that exist among healthy families, schools that educate, and productive workplaces.

Simple enough to say, so very difficult to do—for this will require a complete reorientation of the thinking of educators and society in general about school and the process of transmitting knowledge and skills to learners.

The Experience of Vocational Education

LUCKILY, there is an experience base upon which to draw for this requisite rethinking of instructional strategies: vocational education. When critically analyzed, this experience can be translated into another component of tech prep's conceptual foundation (see Figure 8.1).

To reiterate an important point, tech prep is much more than vocational education, but incorporating the best of the latter is essential to the success of the former. To carry out this important, complex, and difficult task, tech prep practitioners must understand what vocational education is really like today, the dramatic changes it has undergone since 1917 (it *is not* the same program that it was seventy-five or even twenty-five years ago), the reasons for these changes, and the dynamics through which they were brought about. For the most part, these dynamics are internal. Vocational education has always shown a remarkable degree of resistance to change proposed by those outside its ranks.

Inasmuch as tech prep focuses on the population historically targeted by vocational education — the non-baccalaureate bound — it will face similar pressures and problems. If those who lead tech prep understand the evolution of vocational education, especially its internal revolution of the past thirty years, they will not only be able to adopt its most successful strategies and avoid its mistakes, they can also exercise the same critical self-examination and join the leaders of vocational education (and, increasingly, apprenticeship) as they continue the important debates about the place of education-for-work in American schools. This latter task may well be one of their most important roles.

To place themselves in such an advantageous position, tech prep practitioners must have answers to the following questions:

What is vocational education's experience in American education and with this more effective pedagogy (i.e., context-specific and experiential)?

95

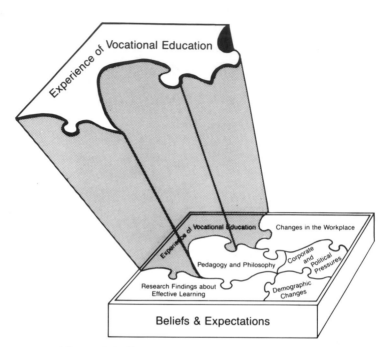

Figure 8.1 *The experience of vocational education.*

What lessons can be learned from this experience that will assist in restructuring schools?

THE CULTURAL HERITAGE OF VOCATIONAL EDUCATION

Although it has been said from the outset that tech prep is not vocational education under a new label or name, it has also been claimed that within its best practices resides a pedagogical and philosophical core that is essential to the success of tech prep. Best practices have been defined as those that open up the options of students, teach them theory as well as specific skills, and motivate them to learn. These kinds of practices can obviously benefit tech prep and any other educational reform strategy.

But if vocational education, which has been on the scene now for some seventy-five years or so, can be this major source of content, methodology, and energy for reforming education, why has such a possibility not become a reality? Why does it continue to be boxed-in and isolated from college preparatory and general education, even in the so-called comprehensive high school? And how can tech prep expect to fare any better, unless it identifies the root causes of the problems encountered by vocational education and learns how to avoid them? An analysis of the many threads that comprise the heritage of vocational education is instructive, for the similarities between its past and tech prep's present and apparent future are many. And Santayana (1905) *was* correct in saying, "Those who cannot remember the past are condemned to repeat it."

Although vocational educators often seem to have boxed themselves in, they have had plenty of help in building the box. The prototypical vocational educator, seen by many as bristling with defensive and isolationist tendencies, did not arrive upon the scene full grown, as it were. Instead, both they and their programs are a reflection of the attitudes and values that most Americans share about the place of work in their individual and collective lives.

America through the 1850s

An understanding of what Americans believe about work (and therefore, what they believe about educational programs that prepare people for work) begins with the roots of Western civilization. Two kinds of people were identified by the early Greek thinkers and philosophers, based upon what they perceived to be a natural division of labor: the "ideal-minded," who dealt best with ideas and ideals, and the "practical-minded," who could work best with the concrete form of an idea, but not its abstraction. This distinction eventually led to the conclusion that those who work with their minds were somehow not only "different from" but "better than" those who work with their hands. The colonial infant that was to become the United States of America cut its teeth on these beliefs, the vestiges of which are still a dominant cultural force in its society.

Since wealth in early America was based primarily upon property ownership, the property owner naturally assumed the prerogatives and responsibilities of the ideal-minded class, employing those who owned no property, planning for and guiding society, and working at becoming cultured. Therefore, they and their children were educated at home by tutors and in early academies and common schools to carry out these

''God-given'' responsibilities. The most formal education was reserved for the elite, specifically the clergy. As for the rest, training for employment followed the ancient route of apprenticeship, a strategy that quickly became institutionalized through governmental policy (Butts, 1955).

This bi-polar approach spawned the dualism that has brought American education to its current state of crisis. The fires in which this differentiated system was being forged were the intrinsic beliefs and attitudes about work held by these first Americans. And, thus, the die was cast for vocational education: it would be the preparation for learning a trade, and it would always be viewed as somewhat less than the very best that society had to offer (Thompson, 1973).

The Land Grant College Movement

Even in the development of the land grant colleges in the early 1860s, a national educational initiative without precedent or parallel to this day, it is clear that these institutions were primarily for those who were of a ''practical'' frame of mind. Without detracting from their contributions (and they are myriad), it is worthwhile to note that the thesis upon which these institutions were founded served to reinforce the notion of a theoretical education for one kind of citizen and a practical education for the other. No matter how this thesis is couched or explained, those who choose (or in the worst case, are placed into) the latter group are always perceived as second class by members of the former group, and alas, at times, they see themselves the same way.

This arrogant and false distinction becomes even more incongruous today, when it is the technically well-prepared who will obtain the high-paying jobs and upon whom society will depend most as it enters the twenty-first century. Yet, for a present-day rendition of this cultural bias, listen to the chants thrown at the students of every land grant institution in this country by their arch-rivals at any athletic event.

Be that as it may, with the success of the land grant colleges, it was only natural that such practical programs would be proposed for the large number of public school students who were not going to reach the collegiate level. And this is exactly what happened through the manual training and the trade school movements during the mid- and late-nineteenth century, but for very different reasons.

Manual Training Schools

In the late 1860s, Professor Calvin Woodward decided that his engineering students at Washington University in Saint Louis should construct models made of wood to illustrate certain mechanical principles. He combined theory and practice in the belief that theory should be of immediate value to the student and that performing a process or experiment was intrinsic to a student's understanding of it (Barlow, 1974).

The philosophy behind the manual training school movement was an attempt to move away from the historic and culturally acceptable division of labor toward a more holistic approach to education. Woodward's rationale was rejected quickly, particularly by the industrialists, but his influence continued in the program known as industrial arts and is emerging, once again, in tech prep.

As for vocational education, the focus remained on the philosophic mainstream that held that only a chosen few can learn theory and the less able need to be taught practical skills and go to work as quickly as possible. Is it any wonder that vocational education became known as a training program that is wonderful for "everybody else's child"?

THE TRADE SCHOOL MOVEMENT AND THE BIRTH OF VOCATIONAL EDUCATION (1890 – 1917)

The educational philosophy framed for vocational education during the period from 1890 to 1917 became the nearest thing to a definitive and explicit statement as has ever been officially claimed by the field. Many diverse groups were involved in the pre-1917 deliberations, each addressing what it perceived to be the most critical problems of the day, although from decidedly different perspectives. Eventually, the philosophy that emerged included portions of all these perspectives, with the possible exception of that of John Dewey (more about this below). Although both the needs of students and the marketplace and, ironically, the resulting vocational education programs themselves changed dramatically over the years, it was not until almost sixty of those years had passed that this philosophy would be seriously questioned by the vocational education establishment itself (Greenwood, 1978).

Many of its early advocates were not reluctant to proclaim their belief that vocational education's function was exclusively economic. But, even in that era of unparalled economic expansion, it was easier to propose that American schools be adapted to the needs of industry than it was to make this a reality. Many people had plenty of reservations about the premise that what was good for business was, in fact, good for America, especially when it came to their schools.

Simultaneously, the schools faced other problems for which there were no easy answers. With the mandate to educate all the children of all the people, which now included a huge number of new immigrants, something had to be done to revitalize education. However, few seemed to agree upon just what that something was. It is not surprising, therefore, that educators of note were found on both sides of the debate about the place of vocational education in the public schools.

The philosophy of John Dewey, which must be analyzed separately, served almost as a counterpoint to much of the rhetoric. Over the years, he has been often quoted regarding vocational education, but his ideas have not been implemented to any real degree in traditional programs. (Interestingly, tech prep brings the debate full circle.) Inasmuch as Dewey represented a truly major attempt in Western civilization to leave the mainstream of philosophic thought, and his view of "holism" contradicted the prevalent "dualism" theory, it is not surprising that his ideas caused a great deal of alarm.

The reader should be advised that, in addition to the rather specific and sometimes narrow perspectives and rationales attributed to each of the groups discussed below, each of them supported vocational education for additional, and perhaps less selfish, reasons. And even though each of the portrayals is something of an over-simplification, pondering them is essential to understanding the philosophic amalgam that has always been vocational education, which is still at work behind the scenes of tech prep.

The National Association of Manufacturers (NAM)

The support of the National Association of Manufacturers (NAM) for vocational education in the late 1800s and early 1900s is particularly instructive. The NAM's founding fathers believed that the economic prosperity of a locality and its business institutions were inextricably linked (see pp. 77–78). Therefore, the way to tell if a proposed policy was good for a locality was to determine its effect upon business in the area (Wirth, 1972).

The NAM promoted vocational education as a major component in its effort to put America in a better competitive position in the world market. Their logic was simple: Germany was the world's leading economic power. Germany had a national policy that supported trade schools. America had all the elements necessary for successful competition, except an established trade school program. Therefore, the addition of vocational education (which to them meant trade schools) was imperative for corporate survival. And in what was for them a logical segue, this translated into vocational education being essential to America's survival as a force for freedom and democracy in the world.

The Labor Movement

Before automation restructured the economy of America, it was in the best interest of the working family to secure employment for all their children as early as possible. Later, however, as working conditions improved, so did wages. But an oversupply of labor, fueled by these same child laborers, tended to keep wages low. So the NAM found an unusual bedfellow in its support of vocational education – the American labor movement.

In vocational education, labor leaders saw a chance to kill two birds with one stone. By delaying the entry of children into the job market, adult workers could experience increased wages *and* the condition of their children could be improved by additional schooling. Most of these parents believed that such schooling would be of more immediate benefit if it were work-oriented. This perception was supported by some leading educators who argued also that the retention power of vocational education on the children of workers seemed to be greater than that of the schools' traditional curriculum.

So organized labor became another strong supporter of vocational education. As was the case with the NAM, their support was based upon an open admission and acceptance of the dualism in American society. And like their NAM counterparts, they wanted to exercise as much control as possible over the employment of persons for the jobs that were available (Thompson, 1973).

The Agriculturists

At the turn of the century, one might have supposed it unlikely that agricultural and industrial leaders would cooperate to secure Federal funding of education. But the political process being what it is, the two did come together in support of vocational education. However, it is important to recognize that the agricultural interests had their own, somewhat different, agenda for changing education, and it was just as complex as that of the industrialists. The subsequent political alignment of the two groups was probably far more complicated than the simple "quid pro quo" suggested below (Swanson, 1979).

But politics did play a major role in establishing vocational education in the schools of America—the industrialists needed the support of the agricultural sector and its political leadership to make their dream of trade schools a reality. Rural lawmakers controlled the Congress and had launched the Federal government into aid to education through the Land Grant College Act of 1862. They had also established the agricultural experiment stations (the second component of the highly successful agricultural extension service delivery model) through the Hatch Act of 1887. And they would soon complete that educational model through the Smith-Lever Act of 1914, which established extension faculties (county agents) of these universities in every county in the country.

One of the most influential agricultural magazines of that day, *Hoard's Dairyman*, provided its editor with a platform from which to speak on educational reform, and Hoard was not reluctant to use this podium. In fact, he did so quite effectively, advocating reshaping the meaning of education to include teaching girls home economics skills, while boys would learn about the application of science and technology to American agricultural production (Wirth, 1972).

The interests of the two groups (industrial and agricultural) in matters of education were so different on a philosophical plane (notice Hoard's emphasis on science and technology) that the programs they spawned (trade and industrial education, and agricultural and home economics education, respectively) have always given evidence of that difference. Yet the two groups needed each other, and so in return for the support of the industrialists for the Smith-Lever Act (1914), rural legislators provided the necessary votes to make the difference in 1917.

Social Reformers

Shortly after the middle of the nineteenth century, a movement emerged to improve the lot of the urban tenement dweller, whose numbers were swelling because of massive immigration. Leading this effort were the settlement house workers, including such notables as Jane Addams, Ellen Gates Starr, and Robert Woods. Their attention was drawn to vocational education for reasons quite different from those of the industrialists, the union leaders, or the agriculturists. They were interested in equipping the upcoming generation with both occupational and *moral* tools, which they believed were required by the evolving industrial system (Woods and Kennedy, 1922; Wirth, 1972). And they were sure that vocational education could help them achieve their goals.

Educational Leaders

Education was under constant attack, seemingly from all sides, and eminent educators were drawn into the affray. They were also concerned with a completely different set of problems, not the least of which was the changing role of the high school: "The influx of working class and immigrant children threatened to destroy the high school's traditional function" (Lazerson and Grubb, 1974, 21−22).

Some thought that training students for specific jobs might answer the harshest criticisms of the industrial leaders and politicians. However, adding vocational education to the high school seemed to contradict the basic belief in a common education for all students (or at least for all those who were fortunate enough to attend schools at that time). The fundamental issue for these persons was the degree to which vocational education would contribute to or impede commonality and democracy in education.

"What emerged was a redefinition of the idea of . . . educational opportunity and a rejection of the common school ideal" (Lazerson and Grubb, 1974, 24). If education for democracy were ever to be a reality in that redefined context, instruction had to be modified and made applicable to the socioeconomic background, needs, interests, abilities, and aspirations of *all* children. From this concept, there developed the differentiation of the curriculum into multiple occupational categories. Therefore, ". . . vocational education was first justified, then glorified, as the only basis upon which a mass educational system could be made democratic" (Lazerson and Grubb, 1974, 25).

John Dewey

Even in these formative days, however, there were those who saw a different and more comprehensive role for vocational education. No one was more visible than John Dewey, whose arguments were described earlier as a counterpoint to the official philosophy of vocational education. Although most of his beliefs were flatly rejected at that time, it is interesting to note that many of the practices of vocational education had quietly evolved in his direction by the mid-1970s.

Dewey saw a potentially dramatic role for vocational education, not only in education, but in the larger American culture. Most educators accepted the nature of technology as a given and tried to accommodate their students to industrialism as directly as possible. Not so with Dewey, who wanted ". . . a kind of vocational education which will first alter the existing industrial system and, ultimately, transform it" (1915, 283 – 284). Recognizing this, one can understand why many industrialists *and* educators were aghast at his opinions and recommendations.

The issue for Dewey was the contrast between adding vocational and technical studies to the curriculum so that students might gain insights into the complexities and value issues of the industrial society *versus* permitting vocational programs simply to train students to serve industry. He preferred the former and fought against the latter, and he was not completely alone. For example, Frank Leavitt asked, "Why should we hesitate to lay hands on industry in the name of education when we have already laid hands on the schools in the name of industry" (1914, 79 – 81).

The question they brought to the table, with all its social, cultural, political, economic, and pedagogical ramifications, was the degree to which the educational system would be *active* or *reactive*. If schools were only to react to the needs of society, then they should be tied to the needs of the business-industrial complex. If, on the other hand, the system were to influence change, schools became obligated to take advantage of the multisensory and practical experience dimensions of business and industry and to demand the use of these as educational resources.

Dewey rejected the narrow concepts he saw emerging, which he felt failed to deal with the all-important value issues (Wirth, 1972). Despite his admonitions, vocational education, as instituted in 1917 and practiced for the next sixty years or so, had little, if any, of his beliefs incorporated into its official philosophy. Instead, it was set upon a narrow path designed by the emissaries of industrialism and the disciples of dualism.

ACTUAL INTERPRETATION OF VOCATIONAL EDUCATION (1917 – 1975)

Ultimately, Charles A. Prosser became the spokesman for vocational education, defining its sole purpose to be that of training for gainful employment. As late as the middle of the twentieth century, he still insisted that all vocational education content should be specific, and that "there must be as many specific courses or groups of courses as there are occupations for which [vocational education] proposes to train" (Prosser and Quigley, 1950, 228).

Prosser was also certain that if vocational education were ever to succeed, its administration could not be left to the general educators, and he fought as long as possible for a separate system. Eventually, he had to compromise, but he still created a framework that permitted vocational education, particularly its administration, to remain a separate entity within the larger educational system. And as the first Federal administrator of vocational education, Prosser enforced his rather narrow, separate, and restrictive philosophy through Federal policy, rules, and regulations (Law, 1975).

[One of the paradoxes of vocational education is that until the mid- to late-1970s, few, if any, state legislatures did any more than write vocational education legislation that permitted the receipt of this Federal money. At the same time, these states were trumpeting the message that education was a state responsibility and that the Federal government should keep its hands off. And even more strangely, these states first matched the Federal funds dollar for dollar (as required), and ultimately "overmatched" them by ratios of as much as eight- and ten-to-one, without any protest about loss of control over that state money. The result was that a relatively small amount of Federal money controlled a much larger amount of state money and kept vocational education on its original narrow track, *whether state leaders wanted it that way or not.* This paradox is worthy of study, in and of itself. However, for purposes of this analysis, let it simply be said that many vocational educators, especially the state directors (see p. 109), were quite content to let the Federal tail wag the state dog. For them, control was the central issue.]

Grant Venn (1964), who attempted to increase the programmatic options of vocational education during his tenure as its Federal administrator, provided a cogent analysis of the rationale behind this early, narrow definition of vocational education. Although it is obvious that Venn did not concur with their approach, he did understand that these early positions had been taken for what Prosser and others believed to be justifiable reasons, based upon their experience with general education and general educators.

One reason Prosser was able to institute his narrow view of vocational education was because the more academically oriented educational leaders of the day were not inclined to get involved. The net result, some seventy-five years later, is the isolation and separation between vocational and college preparatory education that exists in far too many instances. If current day college preparatory educators distance themselves from tech prep in the same manner, the stage will be set for a repeat performance.

In 1917, led by Prosser, the National Society for the Promotion of Industrial Education (NSPIE), with its diverse membership of manufacturers, labor leaders, agriculturists, and social reformers, secured legislation to begin vocational education in America's public schools. And the stroke of the pen that signed Smith-Hughes into law did more than just provide skill development opportunities to millions of American high school students, although, to its everlasting credit, it most assuredly did do that.

THE RESULT: A RETROSPECTIVE VIEW

Through Smith-Hughes, the cultural dualism of American society was formalized within the public secondary schools [i.e., academic education (general and college preparatory) for the elite and training (vocational education) for the less able masses]. Although the education establishment ostensibly accepted vocational education as a legitimate function at that time (they had to in order to receive the Federal funding), this acceptance required no basic review or modification of the beliefs of school, district, state, and teacher education leaders concerning either vocational or academic education. (This is happening again, far too often, as tech prep gains headway.)

As a result, two widely disparate programs began to operate under one roof, figuratively, and at times literally, with separate and sometimes contradictory purposes. In spite of the dreams of those who designed the comprehensive high school, vocational educators and their more academic counterparts tended to grow further and further apart over the years, rather than closer together. Although it is true that physical proximity bred respect and friendship among individual teachers in countless situations; as groups, academic and vocational teachers have always marched to different drummers.

One might hypothesize that the public school leadership of the early 1900s, who for the most part had been brought up under the common school ideology, saw vocational education as a quick and easy solution to the problem of "what to do with all these students who are not college material." It was then but a very short step to the expedient of handing the responsibility for their education over to vocational education. And in vocational educators, they found a group who could not only get the job done, but who reveled in their difference, apparently not realizing that "different" almost always got defined as "second-best" before it was over.

It can also be theorized that the desire of vocational educators to be perceived as completely different from academic teachers and administrators was designed to lead to the two separate school systems that they had earlier been unable to legislate into existence (Wirth, 1972). If this were the case, it did not come to fruition. And the result has been maximum divisiveness and tension between two groups that should and could have been working together. Whatever the reasons, the separation of vocational education and academic education in American public schools was set, almost as if in stone.

The fact that only one philosophical viewpoint—Prosser's—was incorporated into Smith-Hughes is neither good nor bad. Legislation never activates all sides of a philosophical debate. The unfortunate aspect was that Smith-Hughes brought the debate to a close, at least on the surface. Beneath that surface, it continued to boil and manifested itself in the mutual distrust and disdain in which some academic and vocational educators seem to hold one another to this day.

And because the debate was apparently settled, it suggested that the only legitimate subject for future vocational education scholars to pursue would be the improvement of the process as originally defined by Prosser and his peers. (As for academic scholars, no self-respecting vocational educator was going to pay any attention to someone who, obviously, didn't understand vocational education.) And so for more than sixty years, the official vocational education agenda did not encourage any attempt at criticism, external or internal, constructive or otherwise, of its philosophical base (Greenwood, 1978). This early legislative victory also signaled that the political process would be used increasingly by vocational educators as they sought to stake out their position in the educational world. And for most of its life, vocational education has been quite adept at managing this political process, particularly at the Federal level.

One of the results of these two phenomena has been that, over the intervening years, the only statements about the purposes of vocational education to which the vocational education family, as a whole, has been willing to pay much attention have been those embodied in Federal legislation. One might then quite reasonably wonder about the seedbed for the ideas of and motivation behind this large number of Federal legislative enactments, for such major legislation is not spun from thin air (remember the ferment that preceded Smith-Hughes in 1917).

The Source of Federal Legislative Language

A review of Federal vocational education legislation shows that, since Smith-Hughes, it has usually taken its direction from the American Vocational Association (AVA), the state directors of vocational education, or both. The successful lobbying efforts of the AVA are legendary and have often been the topic of conversation in a city known for such activities. It is not surprising, then, that AVA has gained much more fame and is much better known than its sister organization, the National Association of State Directors of Vocational Technical Education (NASDVTE).

Likewise, their different reputations can be attributed to relative size, AVA counting itself one of the largest associations of its kind in the country, while NASDVTE is comprised of the fifty state directors, their staff members, and a few associate members. It is obvious that AVA is the parent organization—every state director is a faithful member, and some are leaders of the larger group. There is also a division of labor of sorts between the two, which results in their tackling different concerns in the name of vocational education. It is this latter difference that is of most interest here.

In recent years, AVA has had to devote itself largely to maintaining and consolidating the gains garnered during its extremely successful early years. Because of the energy and resources required in these actions, it has seldom had the time or inclination to become involved in introspective analysis and criticism of vocational education itself. This should not be surprising, given the diversity within its membership. Typically, the glue that has kept the various components of the organization knit together has been the defense of vocational education, rather than a lot of reflective searching of its soul or attempting to enlarge the venue of vocational education. This assessment does not disparage the AVA—someone has to represent the practical daily interests of the vocational education constituency, and AVA has performed this role in a more-than-exemplary manner.

However, if one goes back to the laying of the field's power base, it will be clear that Prosser put the responsibility and authority to run vocational education into the hands of state boards of vocational education which, in most cases, meant the state director whom that board employed. This has been true, almost without exception, over the intervening seventy-five years. Therefore, in matters of Federal vocational education legislation, it has been these state directors to whom the Congress has listened most, rather than, for example, the chief state school officers who were, in many cases, their official supervisors. To understand the internal dynamics of vocational education change, attention must be given to the activities of these key players.

The 1990 Perkins Act provides some interesting insights into the dynamics of this scenario. Much of its wording is at least inconsistent with, if not diametrically opposed to, the stance originally taken through Smith-Hughes (e.g., integration of academic and vocational education and support for tech prep). Did this dramatic change come about because of outside criticism and pressure? No, the primary roots of the Perkins' language came from the heart of the vocational education establishment itself—the testimony of key state directors of vocational education (U.S. House of Representatives, 1989). If this move toward openness, comprehensiveness, and integration came from that leadership core, then something must have been happening over the years within that group that escaped the notice of most observers.

CHARTING A NEW DIRECTION (1975 –)

As suggested earlier, for the first sixty years or so after Smith-Hughes, almost all of the contributions of vocational educators to the literature dealt with improving that which was already being done. The nearest thing to an analysis of its underpinnings were articles and books on the principles of vocational education.

Melvin L. Barlow (1974), the "Grand Old Man" of vocational education for many years, enumerated some of these principles in an AVA yearbook entitled, somewhat paradoxically, *The Philosophy of Vocational Education*. He was convinced that vocational education's basic principles had been determined, defined, and enunciated between 1906 and 1917. Nor did he believe that they had changed in the intervening years, although he was of the opinion that they had been *reinterpreted* through Federal legislation to keep up with evolving social, economic, and technological conditions (Lee, 1976). Miller, on the other hand, found that "Prosser [himself] did not believe that those principles would [or should] remain unchanged throughout time" (1985, 5).

Whatever the evolutionary pattern of these principles of vocational education may have been, they were ". . . substituted for a philosophy for vocational education [with detrimental effect, because principles] . . . do not equate to a philosophy" (Miller, 1985, 5). And it was the lack of a clear philosophy, or rather, the inconsistency of emerging vocational education initiatives with Prosser's original philosophy that made many vocational educators of the 1960s and early 1970s feel somewhat schizophrenic.

However, it was not until the mid-1970s that any serious questions emerged about the official rationale of vocational education. Stated more correctly, it was only then that such questions emerged in ways deemed legitimate by the field (Greenwood, 1978). The tendency of vocational education to deny the legitimacy of outside criticism was noted earlier and is almost legendary. This time, however, the criticism and questions came from a new and totally unexpected quarter.

In May, 1975, the following challenge was issued by a state director of vocational education to his peers:

I call for a national debate on the role of vocational education in the educational structure, to be led by the best minds in vocational education. Such debate should not center on defending our practices but, instead, should re-evaluate who we are, what we are doing, and, most importantly, why we exist. (Law, 1975, 3)

In response, the National Association of State Directors of Vocational Education (NASDVE) organized a Committee on Philosophy and sponsored a work session for state directors and their key staff members later that same year. At that meeting, the stage was set by the first speaker, who asserted that (Law, 1976, 3):

1) Vocational education has no clear, concise, easily definable philosophical base to which it can lay primary claim.

2) The pseudo-philosophical bases upon which vocational education loosely operates are a conglomerate of beliefs, indiscriminately interwoven, part of which are mutually exclusive and often contradictory.

3) Typically, even the most serious attempts of vocational educators to deal with philosophical issues have resulted in a discussion of surface philosophical tenets . . . rather than in a rigorous philosophical discourse that questions the basic reasons for the existence of vocational education.

Turning his attention to specific sacred cows of vocational education, he further stated his belief that:

4) *True skill salability* is a function both of the mastery of a specific skill for job entry *and* the transferability of that skill for career stability.

5) The very premise of vocational education that has led to its success (i.e., the provision of salable skills for entry-level employment) may lead to [its] demise, if a new definition of salable skills is not derived that includes the intervening variable of transferability.

6) By the year 2000, the most salable skills . . . may be the most theoretical skills.

7) Vocational education has two major functions:
   • The introduction of individuals to true salable skills, which are at least as conceptual as [they are] specific, by starting them with the concrete and moving toward the abstraction, to the degree possible.

- The provision . . . of a salable skill for job entry [which] is an objective attained almost as a spin-off on the way to reaching the major objective mentioned above.

Others (Shoemaker, 1976) were not quite so sure these assertions were valid, and the debate, then and later, was quite lively. Miller (1976, 19) concluded the opening session of the workshop with the following questions:

Will vocational education in the next quarter century be directed by a Smith-Hughes mentality—a mentality perfectly adequate and even far-sighted in the early part of this century—or will vocational education reflect the rate of change and the changes occurring in our society?

The importance of this dialogue was that the major administrators of vocational education were not only sanctioning the debate, they were leading it. For, according to Greenwood (1978, 14):

. . . the recognition of the need for philosophic development and examination could not receive high priority by the field of vocational education until one of the officers of a State Board of Vocational [Education] deemed it essential.

Seeds were also being sown at that conference that would grow to fruition many years later, for example in the intent and wording of the 1990 Perkins Act.

Impeccably credentialed vocational education leaders such as Mary Ellis, a past-President of the American Vocational Association, supported the need for such a debate (Lee, 1976). And in the seventh *Yearbook of the American Vocational Association*, the following question was posed:

Cannot vocational education perform a larger, more important, inherently better function than it presently does, and at the same time lose none of its present effectiveness? (Law and Greenwood, 1977, 95)

By the following year, the vocational education pot had been stirred so much that Greenwood recorded Barlow acknowledging that in his eminent career of writing and teaching, he had only occasionally "nudged against" the philosophical footings of vocational education, and saying, "It is high time that we begin the process of critical review and come to some consensus of what our philosophical base actually is" (Greenwood, 1978, 143 – 144).

In 1979, in one of several "White Papers" commissioned by the Bureau of Occupational and Adult Education (BOAE) in the U.S.

Department of Education, the following national purposes for vocational education were proposed (Law, 1979, 19−20):

1) To support and strengthen the relationship of education to work by encouraging the states to assume the legislative responsibility for vocational education [The late 1970s had seen a number of states pass legislation authorizing their own programs.]

2) To increase national productivity and attain higher employment rates through providing individuals with remunerative skills (both immediate/specific and long-range/transferable) for use in the home and on the job

3) To provide individuals with information about the world of work (as it is and as it should be)

4) To provide all persons equitable access to programs of education-for-work

5) To assist individuals in developing decision-making skills, particularly with regard to work

6) To assist persons who have not mastered the basic literacy skills to do so

7) To prepare persons for advanced vocational and technical education, regardless of the level of that instruction

8) To impact upon the workplace through increased efficiency and improved working conditions

9) To serve as an instrument of foreign policy (inasmuch as the free enterprise system through which American democracy operates, and which vocational education teaches, is a logical product to export)

Although none of these purposes were specifically written into the resulting legislation in 1982, the internal revolution was far from over. In 1984, the National Commission on Secondary Vocational Education said, ''Vocational education is both a body of knowledge and an educational process, but the educational process has not received the degree of attention it deserves,'' and that ''state vocational educators have relied excessively on federal regulations as a substitute for developing a comprehensive educational philosophy'' (National Commission on Secondary Vocational Education, 1984, 19).

In 1985, Mel Miller's long-awaited work, *Principles and a Philosophy for Vocational Education*, set about the task of inferring the principles of vocational education from its practices in what still stands as the major effort of its kind. In a chapter entitled ''Principles to Philosophy,'' Miller provides the only attempt that exists to date to define a philosophy for (or of) vocational education (Miller, 1985).

Regardless, those who were administering the programs at the state level continued to give evidence of the philosophical changes that were taking place beneath the surface. In 1986, Willard Daggert, Director of Occupational Education for the State of New York, proposed that vocational education integrate academic concepts and teach them through vocational applications (Kademus and Daggert, 1986).

Then in 1990, the National Association of State Directors of Vocational Technical Education Consortium (NASDVTEC) issued a critically important position paper entitled, *Vocational Technical Education: Developing Academic Skills*, which included the following statement:

> An integrated partnership [between academic and vocational education] supporting students' varied learning styles is the most effective means of achieving the academic and vocational-technical competence needed in a global economy. (Pedrotti and Parks, 1991, 66)

(It is interesting to note that Darrell Parks, State Director of Vocational and Career Education in Ohio, who was instrumental in writing the NASDVTEC document mentioned above, was also an active participant in the first debates held by the state directors in 1975 on the philosophy of vocational education.)

It is certainly more understandable then, after reviewing the dramatic changes at the very heart of vocational education, why the 1990 Carl D. Perkins Vocational Education and Applied Technology Act emphasized the need for integrating academic and vocational education and authorized funding for tech prep.

CONCLUSIONS

What, then, is to be learned from this historical review of vocational education that can be helpful in the implementation of tech prep?

1) The views that persons hold about vocational education and are likely to hold about tech prep are consistent with the views held by society in general about work.

2) The dualism of colonial days is still apparent in American society,

and thus, in American education, although this does appear to be changing.

3) Those educational initiatives, including tech prep, that educate for work of less than a baccalaureate level will experience the pressures of the system to place them, the students who enroll in them, and those who teach these students in a category of lesser value.

4) Without a clear statement of pedagogy and philosophy to guide it, tech prep will be unable to withstand these pressures and, like vocational education, will find itself set aside into a separate track within the educational system.

5) To keep this from happening will require that tech prep be pedagogically and philosophically understood and embraced by the entire educational system from the outset. This, in turn, requires the identification and promulgation of a common pedagogical and philosophical base, around which all parties may unite.

6) One way to begin to build that common base is to analyze the best practices of vocational education, where the most accurate evidence of the evolving philosophy of vocational educators is found.

7) These practices have changed and grown from being narrow, restrictive, and isolationist at the turn of the century to today, when specific skills are seen as only one part of a holistic educational experience necessary for obtaining and maintaining employment.

8) The philosophy of vocational education that underlies these practices has evolved to where it is hypothesized to be more consistent than inconsistent with that of college preparatory education.

9) Vocational education teachers and college preparatory teachers should focus more on their similarities than on their differences.

10) However, if each group continues to perceive itself as different from the other, they will continue to operate on that perception.

11) Successful integration of academic and vocational education, which is at the heart of effective tech prep, can occur only when the affected participants correct their misperceptions of each other.

12) The most effective way to help them see their similarities is to help them discover that they are committed to a common philosophy of education.

IDENTIFYING AND ACCESSING A LOCAL EXPERIENCE BASE

Vocational educators comprise the single largest group of teachers, administrators, researchers, and teacher educators in America (nationally and locally) with expertise in context-specific and applied teaching-learning situations similar to those found in the workplace. Those who wish to restructure instructional programs to be more applied and context-specific need to learn how to make use of this experience base. And it behooves them to identify vocational educators who do these things well and to treat them as the major resource they can be.

To this point, vocational education and vocational educators have been described in the aggregate, the resulting image more monolithic than is truly the case. Vocational education, like any other major movement has two identities: the identity of the group, which of necessity masks the uniqueness of its members, and the identities of its individual constituents, including their strengths and weaknesses. It is these individual identities that local leaders should explore for assistance in building a tech prep initiative.

To begin this quest, those responsible for planning and implementing tech prep need to answer the following questions:

Is such an experience base (e.g., applied, context-specific, and experiential) available in my school, school district, and postsecondary institution? If so, how can we take advantage of this experience?

Putting Concepts into Practice: Identifying and Building upon Local Vocational Education Resources

The following activities may be helpful:

1) Get to know everything possible about your vocational education teachers. There are any number of methods you can use (review their records, conduct surveys, ask them to respond to questionnaires, talk with their peers, etc.) to determine their:
   - educational experience, including short courses, seminars, internships, military training, and staff development (outside as well as inside education)
   - work experience, including part-time and summer jobs
   - most effective teaching strategies (ask them to identify and define)

- curriculum development experience
- adult education experiences (Have they taught adults?)
- vocational student organization experience (focus on how they use VSOs as instructional strategies, and stay away from contests, for the most part)
- most successful cooperative activities with their academic peers (and their least successful) and the reasons for the success or failure
- use of co-op work experience with their students
- use of cooperative learning strategies in their classrooms
- experience in identifying and validating competencies and competency test items
- experience in working with advisory committees
- experience in analyzing local communities
- other important characteristics you may identify as your local needs become more clear

2) Identify those teachers whose characteristics suggest their ability to:
- organize instruction to open up career options for students, teach them theory as well as specific skills, and motivate them to learn
- understand the theoretical and conceptual basis of their area of specialization, as well as the specific skills needed for entry-level employment
- put aside divisive thinking and cooperate with their academic peers
- work with the community (business, industry, and citizens in general)
- see the bigger picture of comprehensive education and educational reform
- work well with and teach other adults (peer teachers)
- understand the theory (pedagogy and educational philosophy) that underlies their best instructional strategies
- communicate well in both written and oral formats

3) Organize these individuals into task forces that focus on topics important to the success of tech prep, such as:
- identifying and understanding community needs (labor market and others)

- identifying and understanding the academic and technical skills needed for success in the workplace
- understanding and explaining the use of experiential, context-specific instruction to teach long-term transferable (conceptual) skills
- motivating students through student organizations, cooperative learning experience, outcome-based education, and other innovative instructional strategies
- using the workplace as a learning site, including providing staff development to the workplace supervisors in their role as teachers of the student-worker

4) Provide staff development to the task force members to help them understand their assignment and how to identify and unleash the inherent power of their pedagogy.

One of the problems is that these teachers often know more than they know that they know. As a result, they are not even aware of the instructional power resident in their expertise, and most assuredly, they do not know how to communicate this power to their peers. *This is a critical step in the process:* they must learn how to communicate what they know and do well in a manner that is acceptable to and accepted by their more academic peers.

5) Bring some carefully chosen academic counterparts of these task force members into the dialogue, initially as sounding boards, and fairly quickly as full-fledged members of the task forces. Provide the academic personnel with the staff development necessary for them to understand their role and release the power within their own successful practices. Remember, the pedagogy and philosophy of effective tech prep must ultimately be built of both successful vocational education *and* academic components.

6) Enlarge the original responsibilities of the task forces to include developing strategies and plans for sharing their resident expertise with the entire faculty and staff in the system.

7) Identify the physical resources of vocational education that exist in the system that may offer instructional opportunities for tech prep students (e.g., laboratories, equipment, farms, and greenhouses). Work with the responsible vocational education personnel to devise ways of sharing these resources that contribute to the instructional objectives of both tech prep and vocational education.

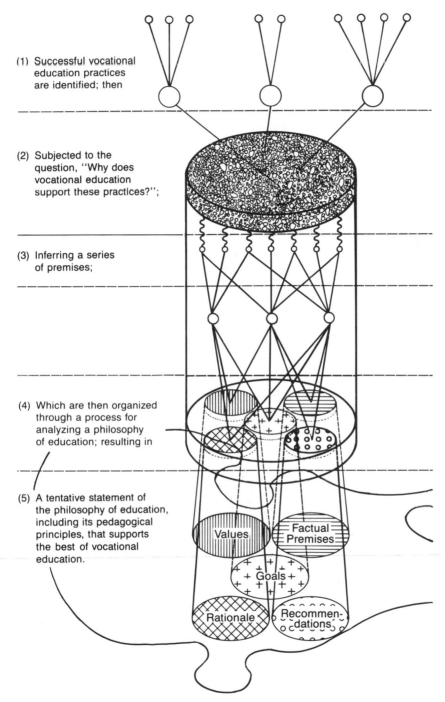

(1) Successful vocational
education practices
are identified; then

(2) Subjected to the
question, "Why does
vocational education
support these practices?";

(3) Inferring a series
of premises;

(4) Which are then organized
through a process for
analyzing a philosophy
of education; resulting in

(5) A tentative statement of
the philosophy of education,
including its pedagogical
principles, that supports
the best of vocational
education.

Values

Factual
Premises

Goals

Rationale

Recommen-
dations

Figure 8.2 *Inferring the pedagogy and philosophy of the best of vocational education.*

8) Use appropriate vocational education and academic facilities (e.g., area career education centers, innovative laboratories, private sector workplaces, and postsecondary institutions) as teacher-training sites.

9) Use the task force members (academic and vocational) as ''teacher trainers'' to instruct other faculty members in methodologies that are consistent with your vision of tech prep.

MAKING MAXIMUM USE OF THE EXPERIENCE OF VOCATIONAL EDUCATION

As the remaining component of the conceptual foundation of tech prep is constructed in Chapters 9 through 11, the misperceptions that have existed between academic and vocational education begin to be erased. This takes place in two steps:

Step 1. Inferring the pedagogy and philosophy that guides the most effective practices of vocational education

Step 2. Modifying the resulting statement to accommodate the differences between vocational education and tech prep

Step 1 (see Figure 8.2) is presented in two parts. Part 1 is presented in Chapter 9 and Part 2 in Chapter 10, while the second step is taken in Chapter 11.

The Philosophy of the Best of Vocational Education — Part 1

RATIONALE

IF it is true, as has been argued, that the core of successful tech prep will include the pedagogy and philosophy behind the most effective practices of vocational education, why is it not enough just to identify these practices? Cannot they then be shared with the rest of the educational world? If they are as effective as claimed, won't others be attracted to them and adopt them for their own use? Why must the additional (and difficult) step of defining these practices pedagogically and philosophically be taken?

Experience shows that some academic educators will not accept or use vocational education practices in their classrooms, no matter how effective they may be for vocational educators. Part of the reason may be image-related: "Just because it works for your vocational students doesn't mean it will work for my more advanced students," a reiteration of the dualism that continues to present itself. More importantly, *as long as vocational educators depend solely upon their practices to explain and define themselves, as they have since 1917, both groups will focus on their apparent differences, rather than search for their commonalities.*

The following example may offer some insight: suppose an English teacher and a vocational agriculture teacher are discussing a student who is enrolled in both their classes, but is doing poorly in English composition. The vo-ag teacher is somewhat surprised because this student has recently done quite well in an FFA Public Speaking Contest, having researched, written, and presented her speech on the topic, "The Effects of Electrostatic Spraying and Dusting on Cotton Production," before a panel of judges and approximately 500 of her peers.

When the agriculture teacher suggests that the student may have been motivated through her FFA activities, he is describing an instructional strategy that has been effective for him and thousands of his counterparts for the past three-quarters of a century. And he is talking about what his experience says is a *curricular* activity. But when his English counterpart hears "student organization," she immediately thinks "extra-curricular" because, in her experience, working with student clubs has always been an activity that went beyond her classroom teaching responsibilities and seldom had instructional implications.

These two teachers have now reached an impasse. Each is trying to understand and assist the other to help a student in whom both are interested, but they are not communicating. And the more the vocational agriculture teacher tries to explain how he uses his student organization to motivate students, help them set their own learning goals, and give them increasing responsibility for establishing their own instructional agenda, the more he reinforces his English counterpart's perception that they are, indeed, worlds apart as teachers.

Before they can communicate clearly, they must establish a relationship based upon a common set of beliefs about the nature of teaching and learning. This common ground can only be reached by both explaining *why* they do what they do with their students. And they can do this best by going beneath (or rising above) their area of specialization and coming to grips with their own pedagogy and educational philosophy. They can then reach a whole new level of understanding about each other and each other's instructional program. On this newly discovered common ground, their assumed differences will begin to disappear, and they will discover that they are much more similar than dissimilar. Then, and only then, can they begin to pool their diverse resources for the benefit of their students.

Ultimately, the core of effective tech prep must include the pedagogy and educational philosophy that guides the most effective practices of both vocational *and* college preparatory education. But one must start somewhere, and in this instance, the process begins with vocational education. However, it must not end there, and *those who struggle with clarifying their pedagogy and educational philosophy as they formulate their own tech prep initiatives should treat what is presented on the following pages as a point of departure only.*

DEFINITIONS

The following definitions guide this search:

Pedagogy—"The art, practice, or profession of teaching; especially systematized learning or instruction concerning principles and methods of teaching." (Webster, 1986)

Philosophy—"A mode of thought that analyzes one's presuppositions and assumptions in every field of thought." (Hook, 1967, 21)

Philosophy of Education – Any philosophy dealing with or applied to the process of . . . education and used as a basis for the general determination, interpretation, and evaluation of educational problems having to do with objectives, practices, outcomes, child and social needs, materials of study, and all other aspects of the field. (Good, 1959, 395)

ORGANIZING THE SEARCH

How, then, does one go beyond the most effective practices of vocational education to their underlying pedagogy and philosophy?

In this case, the steps taken are based upon the premise that a person's pedagogy and philosophy are always evidenced through their consistent practice. This is particularly true for vocational educators, who have historically prided themselves on being action oriented and dismissed anything that smacked of the theoretical. These steps include:

1) Identifying the most effective practices of vocational education (i.e., those that open up the career options of students, teach them theory as well as specific skills, and motivate them to learn)

2) Using these practices as lenses through which to view the pedagogic and philosophic convictions of those who have promoted and implemented them. Keep asking, "Why have vocational educators supported these practices so strongly for so long?"

3) Inferring the deeper-level premises or beliefs that underlie these practices through a review of the writings of vocational education practitioners, leaders, and friendly critics

Using such selected practices as the basis for explicating the beliefs that guide the field makes a great deal of sense, for "experience has [always] been 'king of the hill' in vocational education" (Miller, 1985, 3). In fact, Miller, himself, used similar practices as a primary source for identifying more than two dozen contemporary principles of vocational education. Calling his inductive strategy an "inside-out" approach, he compared it to ". . . practicing one's way into a philosophy of vocational education" (1985, 9). [Once again, it must be pointed out that this approach to establishing a philosophy of education, although quite satisfying to practitioners, is incomplete and requires a thorough review, analysis, and revision (if necessary) through more traditional and academically acceptable methods of philosophic inquiry].

The steps taken in this chapter (see Figure 9.1) are similar to Miller's. There is also a great deal of similarity between the principles he inferred and the premises distilled here. However, Miller's emphasis was more on identifying the principles than organizing them into an explicit philosophy statement. Such a statement, tentative though it may be, is presented in Chapter 10 and, not only validates Miller's work, but extends it in ways useful to practitioners.

However, the myriad practices of vocational education do not lend themselves to individual analysis. For purposes of organization, these practices are grouped into bundles through which to manage the task. This is accomplished by identifying distinctive features of vocational education that its adherents believe to be important and within which it is anticipated that most of their practices will meet the criteria of "best." The features selected for this analysis have been emphasized by vocational educators over the years and continue to elicit an immediate and positive reaction from most of them. For lack of a better metaphor,

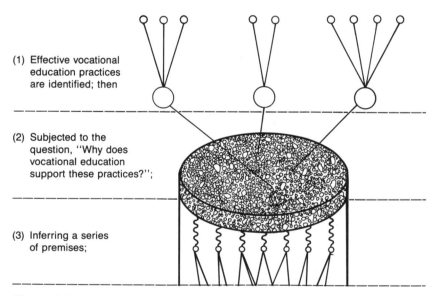

Figure 9.1 *Inferring the pedagogy and philosophy of the best of vocational education—Part 1.*

they are somewhat like buttons that, when pushed, cause vocational educators to light up.

Nine such features (or "buttons") have been identified and provide entry points for this exercise:

1) Skill development
   - on-the-job training
   - cooperative work experience
   - individualized instruction
   - student assessment
   - technical education
   - job placement and follow-up
   - postsecondary education and lifelong learning
2) Curriculum content
3) Community-based education
   - community needs
   - community involvement
   - advisory councils
4) Teacher competency
5) Vocational student organizations
6) The motivating influence of vocational education
7) Occupational choice
8) Programmatic separation or integration
9) Vocational education and the economy

It is important to remember that the practices upon which this analysis focuses are not, themselves, of primary importance. If the reader wishes to learn more about any or all of them, the vocational education literature is replete with explanatory and descriptive material. Instead, they serve as devices through which the pedagogic and philosophic convictions of persons who have spoken for and about them are viewed. Understanding the deepest convictions of these advocates and friendly critics is the goal of this exercise and, ultimately, is more important than understanding the practices themselves. It should also be noted that the synoptic reviews of literature presented to explore each feature are not only selective, they are greatly abridged. Some may charge that such selectivity and brevity is not a valid basis for the inferences reached. For those who disagree with the conclusions reached, for these or other reasons, the challenge is to use this process or a similar procedure to improve upon that with which they take offense.

THE PREMISES OF EFFECTIVE VOCATIONAL EDUCATION

Skill Development

The nation's need for a skilled workforce is central to both past and current vocational education rhetoric and Federal legislation. It was a major feature of Prosser's original proposals and appears often in the literature. However, many strategies have been designed to help students develop the requisite skills. An analysis of seven of the most important of these strategies is presented below.

On-the-Job Training

"The oldest and still the most pervasive way of providing vocational education in every country is through on-the-job instruction" (Evans, 1979, 10). On-the-job training (OJT) is just what the name implies — training received while working in a real job. Although it is seldom used in school-based programs, it is important to understand what vocational educators believe about this practice. For example, by reviewing what they have said and written about OJT, much can be inferred about their views on the workplace as a training site.

Post-employment training is present in all jobs, from the lowest skilled level to the corporate executive. Even when formal instruction has been given prior to a person's being employed, additional training usually occurs once they start work. This instruction is provided in many different ways, including trial and error and through imitation of skilled workers. In its most highly developed format, OJT is carefully designed instruction delivered on the work site by persons who are competent both as instructors and as practitioners of the occupation (Evans, 1979).

Although the use of the job setting as a training site is indigenous to some of the practices of vocational education, there is a point at which a line is drawn between the responsibility of publicly supported education and the employer for such training. If the training required is specific to a particular plant and its environment, it is usually not within the purview of institutionalized vocational education (Evans, 1979). Ginzberg warned those who would give training too specific to a particular job: "If occupational courses teach youngsters how to do very specific things that the employer ought to teach his employees, it is wrong to take time [and other limited resources] for such instruction" (1977, 24).

As new possibilities for restructuring schools are explored [e.g., the high school apprenticeship programs being suggested by the Clinton administration and the cognitive apprenticeship approach favored by Berryman and Bailey (1992)], the line between instruction that is the responsibility of public education and that which employers must provide will become increasingly indistinct. In such cases, coordination and cooperation in planning, delivering, and evaluating the instructional experience will become a higher priority than ever before.

From this brief review of the literature related to on-the-job training, it can be inferred that *most vocational educators believe:*

1) Using the workplace as a training site can be an important component of a skill development program.

2) The more specific the skill to be learned, the more appropriate the use of the actual job experience for training.

3) As skills become more enterprise-specific, society's responsibility for providing such skills decreases.

4) The use of the workplace as a training site should be coordinated by the teacher and take into account the needs of the student and the employer.

Cooperative Work Experience

Cooperative education may have had its origins in England in the nineteenth century, when studies of factory-employed children showed that they were learning as much as other children, although their instructional time was cut in half due to their work loads (Evans, 1971). And much information can be found in the literature that supports the use of cooperative work experience in teaching employable skills. At least two vocational education programs, Marketing Education (Distributive Education) and Industrial Cooperative Training, use co-op work experience almost exclusively. In addition, most vocational education programs are increasing their use of this instructional methodology.

Cooperative work experience embodies the best of the educational and business/industrial worlds. It places students in learning situations in the workplace, but always under the supervision of trained educators. The student's work activities are governed by a training plan and an agreement signed by the student, the employer, and the co-op coordinator. Although the students do earn, the emphasis is on what they learn. A secondary, but by no means unimportant, benefit is the involve-ment of the employer in educational activities. Most successful coopera-tive work experience programs find that employers who get involved with students, in turn, become supporters of the school and continue to participate year after year.

However, Wirtz (1977), a long-time advocate of cooperative educa-tion, felt that too much responsibility for the success of such programs has been placed on education and too little assigned to workplace managers. And in another instance, he seemed almost clairvoyant when he spoke about this type of joint education-work experience being essential to the success of education:

> . . . if the educational system continues to try to discharge alone . . . and by a traditional curricular offering . . . the responsibility of getting every young person up to his or her career entry point, the most likely prospect is that the schools won't succeed in doing this and that they will be blamed even more than they have been in the past for not doing their job. (Wirtz, 1976, 4)

Most students (and, not unimportantly, their parents) and employers evaluate cooperative education as highly successful, when it is practiced properly (Thompson, 1973). Cooperative education has also proven to be effective in terms of placing students in the permanent workforce: many graduates find long-term employment with those with whom they were placed as co-op students.

The use of cooperative work experience need not be limited to instruction in job skills. For example, the National Panel on High School and Adolescent Education (1976, 117) reported:

> Cooperative education often helps to make academic studies more relevant and rewarding for students and to improve self-perceptions and expectations by enabling youth to see what they are capable of doing.

Vocational educators have practiced cooperative education suc-cessfully for many years. There is sufficient evidence to infer that *most vocational educators believe:*

1) Education is bound neither by geography nor time.
2) Students learn through all their experiences, not just those that occur in a classroom.
3) The most effective environment for learning is one that is as true-to-life as possible for the student.
4) Each student should practice the competency in question immedi-

ately and sufficiently to maximize the retention of what they are to learn.

5) Each student must be able to apply that which is being learned immediately.

6) The school's instructional program should complement the learning experiences available in the community, and all such experiences should be coordinated for the benefit of the student.

7) Careful planning on the part of the student, teacher, and employer should precede a student's cooperative work experience.

8) The schools are not totally responsible for the education of their students; other societal institutions share in that responsibility.

9) Many persons, in addition to baccalaureate-degreed teachers, are capable of providing instruction to students.

Individualized Instruction

Vocational education and individualized instruction are not strangers. If one is to teach students to master the skills needed on the job, then it is probably true that, due to the nature of some of the skills, instruction can be provided best in a one-on-one situation. Given the diversity inherent in the typical vocational education student population, such an instructional approach also provides effective options for the different learning styles and capabilities of these students. Although ''vocational education did not invent individualized instruction, it developed the concept thoroughly as an integral part of [its] instruction'' (Barlow, 1974, 21−22).

Franklin J. Keller, who served as the principal of the High School of Performing Arts in New York City, was so enamored of this individual orientation of vocational education that he used the words, ''The Primacy of the Person,'' as the subtitle for one of his books. ''Keller viewed vocational education not as preparation for life, but as life itself'' (Barlow, 1974, 4). In a strong argument that is consistent with Keller's views, Evans (1979) suggested that one of vocational education's purposes is that of ''adding value,'' individual by individual, through identifying and making employable persons who otherwise would not be.

There is substantial data that supports the need for individualized instruction, and few people disagree with the concept (National Panel on High School and Adolescent Education, 1976). It seems firmly imbedded in education, in general, and vocational education, in particular. For example, Evans talked about "a variety of paths to school success [which] capitalize on individual differences rather than trying to force all individuals into a common mold" (1971, 150). And Hruska (1974) argued that this type of instruction is necessary, if the comprehensive high school is to succeed.

From this review and analysis of positions taken by vocational education advocates on individualized instruction, it can be inferred that *most vocational educators believe:*

1) Students are individuals who learn in different ways.
2) Each student is important and must be treated with respect.
3) Students can make a contribution to their own learning experiences.

Student Assessment

It is logical to assume that if vocational educators are interested in individualized instruction, they will be equally interested in determining the degree to which students master the competencies being taught. Not surprisingly, therefore, the accepted instructional model in vocational education includes job analysis, competency identification and validation with employers and employees in the field, using instructional modules to help students master the competencies, and *competency testing.*

In truth, vocational education has led the way in competency-based instruction in American education, referred to within the field as competency-based vocational education (CBVE). "CBVE starts with certain achievable and required competencies and then measures them to see if they have been acquired" (Schaefer, 1979, 68 – 69). Programs of vocational competency testing operate in many, if not most, states, and consortia [e.g., the Vocational Technical Education Consortium of the States (V-TECS)], have been organized so that member states can share in the task and cost of identifying and validating student competencies and establishing test item banks.

Although vocational education was involved in student assessment earlier than most, by the mid- to late-1970s, much of American education was moving in this direction. And by the end of the decade, the competency testing movement had ". . . exploded on the education scene . . . with a ferocity unmatched by some of the most popular educational fads of earlier decades" (Spady, 1979, 20).

It might appear that the widespread criticism of the 1980s pushed a reluctant educational establishment into this kind of performance testing, but the evidence suggests otherwise. For example, Thompson reported in the early 1970s that "the emergent school is committed to exploring new systems of evaluation" (1973, 197). And, in 1976, the National Panel on High School and Adolescent Education suggested that student evaluation should emphasize performance outcomes as well as ". . . the application of knowledge, the recall of knowledge, and college bound academics" (1976, 36). Ferrin, writing for the College Entrance Examination Board went even further by recommending that ". . . the state legislature[s] or governor[s] should establish a state-level inter-agency Career Competency Assessment Board that would report to the highest levels of state [leadership]" (1975, 40).

(It should be pointed out that if competency testing is conceived of as a hard and fast numerical measure of success, then this feature of vocational education may be inconsistent with the holistic approach of continuous progress management advocated by Deming and total quality education. If, on the other hand, such measures are viewed as general outcomes of significance, then the inconsistencies are greatly diminished.)

Based upon the support given by vocational educators to competency testing of their students, it can be inferred that *most vocational educators believe:*

1) Vocational educational programs should result in measurable outcomes that reflect the level of skill attained by each student.

2) Students have the right to know their level of skill proficiency.

3) Education is responsible for providing students with statements of their level of achieved proficiency.

4) The competencies to be taught and the criteria for success should be shared with the student at the beginning of the instructional experience.

5) The performance criteria used should be valid and reliable measures of competence.

6) Vocational education can and should demonstrate its effectiveness through the competency testing of its students.

7) Vocational teachers can and should be evaluated on the skill levels attained by their students.

Technical Education

The term, "technical education," has appeared increasingly over the years in the rhetoric of vocational education. It is now preferable in many quarters to refer to vocational-technical education, rather than just vocational education. In truth, the postsecondary role of vocational education cannot be understood unless the concept of technical education is discussed.

Technical education is a level, more than a type, of education and is needed by the top subprofessionals in any occupational field (Evans, 1971). Technical curricula incorporate basic mathematics and science, as well as the job-related and practical knowledge requirements of a cluster of specific occupations (Thompson, 1973). There is little doubt that most believe technical education to be the core of effective postsecondary employment training programs. And some are beginning to argue that entrance into technical education should not be restricted to postsecondary education (tech prep is a good example of this argument).

Venn was in the vanguard of those who supported this special kind of education (technical education) to deal with emerging technology, and Bundy said as early as 1972 that ". . . it is new technology and cybernation that place new demands on workers" (Miller, 1985, 35). The author (1975) called attention to the increasing importance of technological change, when he hypothesized that a person's ability to adapt to a new job requiring new skills was a proper measure of that person's usefulness to society. In like manner, Kademus and Daggert proposed that vocational education should help students learn basic skills ". . . that will enable them to adapt quickly to the changing requirements of new technologies and to benefit from lifelong education and retraining opportunities" (1986, 13–14).

Technical education, then, is a legitimate extension of vocational education, but its evolution is rooted more in the broader concepts of the changing workplace than in traditional vocational education course offerings. It requires the integration of vocational skills and academic concepts, and it teaches the underlying theories of industrial and business processes, along with emphasizing the performance of specific skills. In fact, the most accessible route to the necessary conceptual skills for most students is through the "hands-on" specifics of technical education's instructional methodology.

It is easy then to infer that *most vocational educators believe:*

1) There is a career ladder within an occupational field that runs from the semi-skilled to the technician and the professional.

2) Vocational education content should be structured to provide exit and re-entry points for students, according to their needs and interests.

3) Vocational education is responsible for providing students with specific job-entry skills.

4) The more technical the job requirements, the more there is a need for the student to possess a conceptual understanding.

5) The more conceptual the nature of the skill, the more likely it is to be transferable.

6) Students can be led through specific low-skill activities into the conceptual by skilled teachers as concepts are grasped.

7) Academic and vocational education subject matter should be integrated into a more holistic instructional program.

8) There should be a meshing or articulation of secondary and postsecondary vocational education curricula, so students can move easily from one level to the other.

Job Placement and Follow-Up

"Placement in the next step [postsecondary education or employment] is a responsibility of vocational education" (Miller, 1985, 51). The corollary to that principle so common to much of vocational education adds, "[and] follow-up is a vital extension of [the process]" (Miller, 1985, 167). And so it is. Job placement and following the careers of graduates to determine their eventual job success have long been practices to which most vocational educators subscribe allegiance.

Struck was one of the very first to urge his peers to accept the responsibility of placing students into jobs for which they had been trained (Miller, 1985). And during the 1960s, Venn promoted job placement assistance for *all* high school-age youth in the school district, not just vocational education graduates. He believed that "job placement is more than a demonstration of program success—it is [a] moral commitment [to the student]" (Miller, 1985, 52).

The Education Amendments of 1976 required a follow-up evaluation to determine the effectiveness of vocational education programs. It would appear, therefore, that members of Congress believed that there was a direct relationship between the placement of graduates into jobs for which they were trained and the effectiveness of vocational education. Recognizing the way in which the political process works, it is more likely that some influential vocational educators convinced key congressional staffers that such a relationship exists. And that influence could have come from almost anywhere in the ranks of vocational education, for:

> Vocational educators are nearly unanimous in accepting job placement as a responsibility, and the placement of graduates in the occupations for which they are trained has always been considered the most tangible measure of the success of vocational education processes. (Leighbody, 1972, 15)

By the mid-1970s, others were becoming concerned about the effect of schooling on job acquisition and the transition from school to work. Writing for *Fortune* magazine, Guzzardi noted that ". . . the first really critical passage comes when teenagers make the hesitant and painful transition from school to work" (1976, 125). And Wirtz (1976) argued, once again, that the responsibility for assisting teenagers through this transition should not be placed entirely upon the schools. The National Panel on High School and Adolescent Education (1976) agreed, recommending instead, the creation of a community career education center to help students take this all-important step.

At about that same time, the College Entrance Examination Board (CEEB) began to promote placement offices in schools on the premise that such an office has as much to offer a school's faculty in terms of information with which they can improve instruction as it does to the students being placed (Ferrin, 1975). For according to Evans, the placement office serves as a feedback mechanism for adjusting ". . . the content and methods of the vocational training program to meet local labor market needs" (1971, 183).

So much for job placement. Why do vocational educators swear a similar allegiance to follow-up? Most often, the reason given is to evaluate the effectiveness of vocational education programs, the premise being that if students do not find employment in the area for which they have been trained, then their instructional program is either inappropriate (not based upon real job demand) or ineffective (does not teach the actual competencies required for the jobs that are available). The College Entrance Examination Board was obviously interested in both of these dimensions of the problem when it recommended that schools conduct annual studies of the progress of secondary and postsecondary school graduates and dropouts who did not immediately continue their education to identify the extent and nature of the misalignment between education exit requirements and work entry requirements (Ferrin, 1975).

From this analysis of the support given the placement and follow-up of vocational education students, it can be inferred that *most vocational educators believe:*

1) The placement and follow-up of students serves as one means of evaluating the effectiveness and integrity of vocational education instruction.

2) Although a placement service meets a vital need of students and their employers, its educational value is in its potential for redirecting instruction.

3) The educational enterprise cannot and should not take full responsibility for helping students make the transition from school to work.

Postsecondary Education and Lifelong Learning

Most vocational educators believe that their students should continue their education, particularly that of a technical nature, beyond the high school. "The level of education for many occupations demands a technical education program which begins in the high school and continues for two or more years beyond" (Evans, 1971, 183). Barlow, in referring to the work of the Panel of Consultants on Vocational Education in the 1960s, said, ". . . it was obvious that modern implementation of vocational education required programs in post-secondary institutions" (1976, 4).

Therefore, it is not surprising to find that "lifelong learning is promoted through vocational education" (Miller, 1985, 31). Even in the very earliest days, David Snedden, a contemporary of Prosser, proposed ". . . short courses, some of which could be highly specialized in nature, for workers already in industries, and [felt] that short courses for farmers might [also] be worthwhile" (Miller, 1985, 31). Venn recommended that continuing education for *all* citizens become an additional cornerstone of America's educational policy, arguing that any individual should be able to ". . . obtain additional general education and new occupational

skills, regardless of previous education or occupational competence''
(1964, 159).

Swanson and Kramer (1965) identified the need for workers to give
increased attention to updating and changing their skills to remain
employable. Then apparently well ahead of their time, they called for
better articulation between high school and postsecondary programs, a
theme that would reappear during the mid-1970s. Ultimately, this idea
would become a central premise of tech prep (i.e., "2 + 2" and "4 +
2" programs of study).

It is clear, then, that a commitment to postsecondary education and
lifelong learning is part of the credo of vocational education. Why? For
one reason, due to an ever-increasing technology, the secondary school
is unable to transmit all the information that the learner needs prior to
his/her graduation (Evans, 1971). And Barlow put his finger on another
when he said, ". . . preparation [for a skilled job] should be given as
closely as possible to the time of [its] use" (1976, 5). From a strictly
economic point of view, Levitan (1977) argued that relating a training
system as closely as possible to an employer (in time as well as in
distance) provides a quicker (and more accurate) response to a changing
labor market.

The commitment of most vocational educators to postsecondary
education and lifelong learning appears to be based upon *their belief that:*

1) Vocational education instruction should be available to all citizens,
   youths and adults alike, at times they need it most.
2) Workers will experience an increased need for retraining
   throughout their careers due to rapidly increasing technology and
   its effect upon their jobs.
3) Specific vocational education instruction should be provided as
   nearly as possible to the time when such instruction is applicable
   to the job needs of the individual.

Curriculum Content

Taking quite seriously the message embodied in their name, vocational
educators have made it clear from the beginning that their purpose is to
train and educate for work. And by that, they typically meant work that
required less than a baccalaureate degree for entry-level employment.
So it is not surprising that, since 1917, vocational education has drawn

upon the blue-collar workplace as a major source for curriculum content, and that "curricula for vocational education are derived from requirements in the world of work" (Miller, 1985, 117).

Prosser thought vocational curricula should be designed only for specific occupations. One of his contemporaries, Charles Allen, promoted curriculum content based solely on the skills needed in a single, identifiable job. As far as he was concerned, these skills were ". . . primarily associated with operating machines and manipulating tools and objects" (Pucel, 1990, 159). This perspective led vocational educators to focus almost exclusively on the competencies needed for performing a particular job as the appropriate content of any curriculum designed to train persons for that job.

Vocational educators also have a distinctive concept of the learner, which leads them to incorporate requisite job skills into the curriculum: "All students must have a goal toward which they direct their activity if learning is to be meaningful," and they ". . . will not be motivated by abstract activities that are inserted to facilitate learning for the sake of learning" (Thompson, 1973, 22). This leads them to the conclusion that "schools should endeavor to have pupils learn things and processes which are of use and value in real life situations" (Thompson, 1973, 22). All these beliefs point vocational educators to instruction that is rooted in the world in which their students live and work.

After a long and rigorous examination of vocational education, the National Commission on Secondary Vocational Education (1984, 13 – 14) came to the same conclusion:

> Curriculum developers in the schools must conceptualize knowledge, devise organizational arrangements, develop instructional methods, and implement administrative procedures that will assure students opportunities to experience the interrelatedness of ideas, the implications and applications of knowledge, and the process of discovery, dissemination, and use of information. The totality of this educational experience can and must be made relevant – to the student and to the real world.

There are many who say that because of this very focus on the workplace, vocational education has been too narrow and has trained its students for obsolescence. Levitan, on the other hand, cautioned that vocational education would be well advised *not* to move completely away from such an approach as it revises its curricula: "The task of vocational educators is to keep pace with changing technology and adjust their course content to current changes in the market place" (1977, 60).

However, much has changed in vocational education since the days of Allen and Prosser. Along with the changes triggered by technology, other expectations have come to the forefront, such as career development and the elimination of sex bias. In addition, questions have continued to be raised over the years about the role of specific occupational training at the high school level (Pucel, 1990).

In the early 1970s, because of these and other concerns, Schaefer and Kaufman (1971, 13) recommended:

> . . . a new arrangement for a large group of students in the "gray" area [the neglected majority?] who will be given a chance to explore the nature of many occupations—an arrangement which demonstrates the inter-relationship among courses and between these courses and future plans, which provides training in broad occupational skills that can be used in a variety of occupations, and, finally, which maximizes the options open to the student after he leaves high school.

Shortly thereafter, Thompson (1973, 152) identified the following minimum requirements for occupational competency in modern American society:

> . . . occupational flexibility, to expect and to know how to seek new employment when his present job becomes displaced, an understanding of job relationships, social compatibility, and a skill that is needed at some place in the world of work.

According to Glenn and Walter, curricular change in vocational education may have just begun. They believe it will be particularly visible in instructional initiatives that emphasize teaching basic academic skills through vocational education courses. Although many practitioners may argue that these skills have always been an integral part of vocational education, in the future Glenn and Walter believe that ". . . teachers [will be] expected to provide specific instruction and remediation [in these skills] for all students" (1990, 100).

Based upon this brief review of the literature on the content of vocational education curricula, one can infer that *most vocational educators believe:*

1) The content of vocational education should have immediate and practical application to the world of work.
2) Vocational education content should be determined by an analysis of the competencies needed for success in the workplace.
3) These competencies should be identified by reviewing current job

activities and making adjustments for predicted changes in the labor market.

4) There is a great deal of commonality among jobs in the competencies that are required for success.

5) Basic academic skills are becoming increasingly important occupational competencics.

Community-Based Education

The literature is filled with statements that suggest vocational education programs are tied closely to the community in which they operate. What does this really mean? What are the tangible results of this commitment? Three subsets of successful community-based educational strategies are identified and analyzed below. Inferences about the beliefs of practitioners regarding these strategies are drawn after the analysis of all thrce, rather than one by one, as is the case in other sections of this chapter.

Community Needs

Vocational education ". . . should be oriented to the manpower needs of the community" (Thompson, 1973, 98). This is a belief that vocational practitioners are likely to voice quickly, as shown above, and so it is not surprising that one of Miller's principles emerged as "[the] needs of the community are reflected by programs of vocational education" (1985, 39). From the very outset, it has been understood that vocational teachers would plan their curricula in cooperation with community employers to ensure its relevance to the workplaces for which they trained (Weatherford and Koeninger, 1974).

However, the definition of community has changed, and vocational education's relationship with that community is also changing. In the past, the community provided the sole basis for curriculum content and the learning experience, as well as job placement after training. However, ". . . the significance of the community has shifted from being the site of both training and employment to being primarily the site of training" (Thompson, 1973, 100).

And while the labor market needs of the community are still important, other more personal needs of the citizens who comprise the community are increasingly being taken into account. ''[There is now] an urgency of looking beyond labor needs to the needs of people'' (Miller, 1985, 41). Wirtz spoke passionately of the need for strong relationships between the school and its community for many reasons, not the least of which was ''. . . to channel constructively the emergent force of increased citizen involvement in community affairs'' (1976, 7).

Community Involvement

A former chief state school officer put the importance of schools getting involved with their communities quite succinctly when he said, ''Incorporating the community into a school district policy-making structure . . . reaffirms the supposition that the schools belong to everyone'' (Scanlon, 1976, 5). He went so far as to recommend that schools take as one of their goals the informing of, as well as interacting and cooperating with, the community, ''. . . finally, arriving at mutually shared responsibility for educating the young'' (Scanlon, 1976, 5).

Weatherford and Koeninger (1974, 220) analyzed a variety of effective vocational education community involvement activities. They then constructed the following basic tenets, which provide a foundation for building a community interaction program:

1) A community interaction program holds enormous potential for meeting the ultimate goals of vocational education.
2) Vocational education will be effective in proportion to the kinds and quality of community interaction [it incorporates].
3) Vocational educators must develop a goal-directed, systematic community interaction program.
4) Society is demanding that education be relevant, realistic, and timely.
5) Community support for vocational education will increase in proportion to the effective involvement of the community.

Advisory Councils

It is impossible to come close to vocational education without coming into contact with its practitioners' dedication to seeking input from their consumers through representative advisory committees. From the group of farmers and ranchers working with a vocational agriculture teacher in a small midwestern school all the way to the now defunct but, at one time, highly prestigious National Advisory Council on Vocational Education, the principle is the same: ''Much of the success of vocational education can be traced directly to effective planning based upon the advice of a variety of representative groups of people'' (Barlow, 1971, 220).

This commitment of vocational educators to advisory groups goes much deeper than merely seeking advice. Through such structures, the interdependency of employer, employee (student), and educator came to be recognized as indispensable to effective programs (Barlow, 1974). And this commitment is so strong that the 1976 Vocational Education Amendments mandated the organization and use of advisory councils at the local, state, and national levels.

(This may or may not have been an appropriate action, but it is a good example of what can occur when the methodology used to implement a concept is given more visibility and importance than the concept itself. For example, it might have been more effective to mandate the involvement and input of affected persons, while identifying advisory councils as one legitimate means of meeting the mandate.)

However, whatever else may be the case, it is clear that the widespread and successful use of advisory groups by vocational educators is a reflection of their belief in involving the community and interacting with their consumers.

From the analysis of these three community-based educational strategies, it can be inferred that *most vocational educators believe:*

1) The schools and their instructional programs belong to the community.

2) The school is accountable to that community for the success of its program.

3) Vocational education teachers can secure valuable input from representatives of the community in instructional decisions.

4) Community members have a responsibility to offer thoughtful and objective advice for improving vocational education.

5) Community members (individuals and institutions) want to become actively involved in schools and have much to offer all of education, particularly vocational education.

6) Meaningful learning experiences occur within the community of which the school is a part.

7) The school should open its doors to the citizens of its community, and, in so doing, open the doors of the community to its students.

Teacher Competency

The requirement that vocational education teachers be *occupationally* competent in the area in which they teach has always set the field apart. From the beginning, the Smith-Hughes Act required vocational education teachers to have appropriate job-related experience, and those who did not were viewed as unprepared to teach. The mindset of the day was "... if you had not earned a living doing something, you probably would not be successful in helping others prepare to earn a living in that occupation" (Miller, 1990, 39).

This perspective was reflected in the very first position taken on teacher competency by the Federal Board of Vocational Education in 1918. After providing assurance that any vocational teacher must, of course, be able to teach, the Board went on to say that competence in the skills to be taught (e.g., carpentry) was the prime requisite and all other qualifications were secondary (Federal Board of Vocational Education, 1918).

However, the most narrow version of that position was short-lived because, "... knowing how to perform a skill did not predispose one's ability to transfer that skill to the student" (Glenn and Walter, 1990, 100). As early as the mid-1930s, there were calls for trade teachers (those most likely to have only a secondary level education) to possess a college degree, in addition to their work experience. Although this did not come about, and the job-competent trade teacher continues as a bulwark of vocational education through what most states call provisional certification, some real changes have taken place.

For example, by the early 1970s, Schaefer and Kaufman (1971, 88) reported a study that set forth the following attributes of a "master" vocational teacher (listed in relative order of importance):

1) Ability to motivate students
2) Knowledge and understanding of objectives of vocational education
3) Knowledge and understanding of the basic principles of learning
4) Experience in the skills of the specialized area being taught
5) Ability to express ideas adequately
6) Ability to demonstrate skills

7) Knowledge and understanding of related technical theory in a specialized area

By this time, the emphasis had shifted to the point that practical experience had become fourth on the priority list, whereas aspects of pedagogy had moved into the first three places. This did not suggest that vocational instruction was to be placed into the hands of workplace novices, but it did suggest that the art of teaching was deemed increasingly important by the field.

This review leads to the inferences that *most vocational educators believe:*

1) Vocational education teachers should have subject-matter mastery, including the specific skills of the occupations in which they teach.

2) Many persons, in addition to baccalaureate-degreed teachers, are capable of providing instruction to students.

3) The necessary pedagogical training should be provided to experienced technicians, so they can perform as professional and competent teachers.

Vocational Student Organizations (VSOs)

Student clubs were first used as instructional tools by some of the early social reformers. They saw clubs, which provided self-discipline and practice in cooperative efforts, when combined with the sense of purpose given by the very nature of trade training, as the touchstone of the new wave in American education (Wirth, 1972). Since that time, "student organizations [have become] an integral feature of vocational education" (Miller, 1985, 75).

The Future Farmers of America (FFA) was organized in 1928, growing out of several state and local organizations related to vocational agriculture. It is quite likely that they, in turn, had been influenced by the early Corn Clubs established by the fledgling Agricultural Extension services, which, in time, would become the 4-H clubs. In 1940, the Future Business Leaders of America (FBLA) was formed, followed by the Distributive Education Clubs of America (DECA) in 1947, Future Homemakers of America (FHA) in 1948, Vocational Industrial Clubs of America (VICA) in 1965, and the Health Occupations Student Association (HOSA) in 1976.

The commitment of vocational educators to their student organizations is the stuff of legend. Theses, dissertations, and articles abound on the topic. In fact, the belief in these organizations is so ingrained in the ideology of the field that one almost risks professional suicide to raise *any* questions about them. Governors' proclamations honoring VSOs, individually and collectively, have almost become a dime a dozen. And in state after state, state boards of education have adopted policies urging local boards to support them as integral parts of instruction.

In many instances, it is difficult to distinguish between the student organization and the instructional program. On the one hand, this can be a positive factor for students and their learning. On the other, it is somewhat confusing and not a little disconcerting to hear the repeated testimonies of young men and women at local student organization banquets that begin with statements that, far too often, go something like this: "When I first started taking FFA (or DECA or VICA, etc.). . . ." The temptation has always been to stop the proceedings and say, "No, you are taking vocational agriculture (or marketing education or automobile mechanics), and your youth organization is just one strategy through which you are learning," for it has appeared, at times, to be a classic case of the cart before the horse.

It is because of the high visibility, overt support, and effectiveness of youth organizations that this instructional strategy was chosen for analysis. It is also because of their high profile that serious questions need to be asked about them before their acceptance as an appropriate methodology is guaranteed. Surely, the advocacy of student organizations by vocational educators is rooted in some deeper pedagogical concepts than appear on the surface; for to say, "I believe in the FFA" (or FHA or DECA, etc.) is not sufficient.

What causes the field to be so strong in its support of these organizations? Is it really an instructional strategy, or has the means truly become the end in this case? What are practitioners after when they promote the use of such organizations?

One commonly stated purpose of these organizations is leadership development: "Leadership development is foremost among the goals of vocational student organizations" (Miller, 1985, 75). Yet nowhere does the Federal legislation list leadership development as a specific goal of vocational education, although it does define vocational student organizations as an effective teaching-learning strategy. It is true that, in recent years, instructional units on leadership have begun to appear in various vocational education curricula. This, however, may be an interesting twist, in which the student organizations have had more influence on the curriculum than the curriculum has had on the student organizations. Since there are no references to teaching students to become more effective leaders in the Federal legislative language of vocational education, and since, as was made clear earlier, there is no other central source document to which most vocational educators go for their definitions and direction, one is led to the conclusion that leadership development is not, in and of itself, a formal goal of vocational education.

The truth of the matter, harsh as it may sound, is that there is no place for vocational student organization activities in a vocational education instructional program, unless they contribute to attaining its instructional goals. While it is hard to envision such things as leadership development being dysfunctional to those goals, every effort should be made to keep student organizations in proper perspective—as one of many strategies to achieve instructional objectives.

Consistent with this perspective, "it was early recognized that some of the goals of vocational [education] could be best promoted through an organization in which students had primary responsibility" (Thompson, 1973, 146). This theme of student responsibility was expanded by Miller when he argued that "people development—helping individuals 'become' is a justification for vocational student organizations" and "motivation toward learning is another outcome of vocational student organizations" (1985, 76). Finally, and most importantly, Miller hit the nail squarely on the head when he said, "Vocational student organizations provide a structure for individualizing instruction in response to the student's interests and needs" (1985, 76—77).

Reel (1979, 217) saw vocational student organizations as the heart and soul of vocational education and as its most effective resource for dealing with the challenges it faces, as well as being vehicles for:

- encouraging students to enroll in vocational education
- providing an informal teaching/learning atmosphere
- expanding experiences and opportunities for vocational education students in the marketplace
- enriching the instructional program with hands-on experience
- motivating students to develop positive self-concepts
- developing [positive] attitudes about social and civil responsibilities
- providing leadership experiences and the opportunities to work effectively with peers and with adults

- meeting and associating with vocational educators, which paves the way for refueling the profession with dedicated, ethical professionals
- providing easy access to and involvement of parents
- publicizing vocational education programs and linking schools with communities

From this discussion and analysis of vocational student organizations, it can be inferred that *most vocational educators believe:*

1) Students are responsible individuals and should be treated as such.
2) If students are given opportunities to exercise responsibility, they will respond accordingly.
3) Students have the right to participate in their own educational process, making some of the decisions concerning both themselves and that process along the way.
4) Self-imposed goals for learning are more useful than goals imposed by others.
5) Many of the actions of students are reflections of teachers' expectations of them.
6) The most effective teaching/learning situation is one that is a model of democracy in action.
7) Education is life, not preparation for life.

The Motivating Influence of Vocational Education

Much has been said recently about the ability of vocational education to motivate individuals and keep them in school. Although some of the rhetoric of the early years made similar claims, in practice, the reverse may have actually been true: "A person had to want to get into the . . . program, his intentions . . . had to be honorable and he had to supply his own motivation to succeed" (Barlow, 1976, 3–4).

Yet, by the early 1970s, among the secondary goals to which most vocational educators subscribed was the belief that:

> Students who have little interest in formal subjects may find these subjects more meaningful when they are taught in relation to occupational goals, and this may encourage them to continue their education. (Leighbody, 1972, 16)

Vocational educators may have been quite glib in their statements on this topic, but there is a research base that supports their assertions. For example, Ellison and Fox reported that ". . . the weight of evidence indicates that vocational courses do make a significant contribution to reducing attrition [of students from the secondary school]'' (1973, 41). And building upon the proposition that learning is enhanced when the students set difficult goals for themselves and when feedback is provided to them as quickly as possible, Evans said, ''Vocational education . . . goals are clear to the student and are related to the real world outside academia'' (1971, 148).

From a purely pedagogical perspective, Jerome Bruner (1973, 105) identified some extraordinarily important connections between vocational education and effective instruction when in answer to his own rhetorical question, *''How can the power and substance of a culture be translated into an instructional form?''*, he responded:

> . . . [by] translat[ing] bodies of theory into a form that permits the child to get closer and closer approximations to the most powerful form of a theory, beginning with [its] highly intuitive and active form . . . and moving on as the child grasps that to a more precise and powerful statement of it.

He called that process education from the outside in. And it is proposed here that ''education from the outside in'' exists in a highly developed state in the best practices of vocational education. For as Hruska (1974, 53) argued:

> . . . vocational education might have more to do with the fascination of materials, the seeking of identity, the relationship of man and things, or in short, the growth and development of people, than with job getting and skill training. . . . Vocational education . . . is a holistic and alternative way of looking at education.

The ability of vocational education to make instruction more relevant for students is probably even greater than has been documented here. Most practitioners believe in its capacity to ''turn on'' kids who otherwise don't seem to learn well. However, little has been made of this potential by persons outside the field. There are notable exceptions. For example, the efforts of Sidney Marland on career education were a move to capture this potential, the SREB projects mentioned earlier are a second, and tech prep now represents another such possibility. Perhaps the chances of tech prep succeeding in this endeavor will be enhanced if the beliefs about the motivating potential of context-specific instruction, such as that found in vocational education, are made more explicit; to wit, *most vocational educators believe:*

1) One of the goals of vocational education is teaching students how to learn.
2) The content of vocational education is more specific than that of general or college preparatory education.
3) Vocational education is visibly applicable to the real world and can make the content of general education more relevant to the daily life of most students.
4) Vocational educators accept students in their current stage of maturity and assist them to grow from that point.
5) Vocational education content should be arranged from the specific application to the general concept.
6) Vocational education is a teaching/learning process that operates best in context-specific situations.
7) Vocational education instruction is experiential in nature.
8) Vocational education, at its best, starts students in the specific and leads them into the conceptual (theoretical) abstraction, as far as each is capable of going.
9) The student who develops conceptual skills can transfer these skills to new jobs as they emerge.
10) Transferable skills are the most salable skills that vocational educators can assist their students to develop.
11) The ultimate aim of vocational education is the learning of transferable conceptual skills.

Occupational Choice

Of all the criticism leveled at vocational education over the years, some of the most damaging has been that it places limits upon the choices individuals can make concerning their occupations or careers. Conversely, there are those who say that education that is so general that it provides *no* salable skills also limits an individual. Between these two extremes there is ". . . a curvilinear function which varies with time, place, and individual characteristics. Vocational education should seek to maximize this function" (Evans, 1979, 8).

Several educational approaches have been designed and strengthened in recent years that help students make more intelligent career choices, and most of these have been supported by vocational education (e.g., career guidance and counseling, career awareness, and career and vocational exploration). Each of these has the same basic objective — helping students learn more about themselves, the world of work in which they live, and how to make the best decisions for themselves in that world. These programs are thought by some to be relatively new to the rhetoric of vocational education, but the need for such activities has long been recognized by the field.

Miller's very first principle, "Guidance is an essential component of vocational education" (1985, 24), was based upon evidence of the influence of early guidance advocates, such as Frank Parsons, on the development of vocational education. And, according to Wirth, "the introduction of vocational guidance into public education was a product of the industrial education movement" (1972, 98). Furthermore, as early as 1921, the newly established Federal Board for Vocational Education gave active recognition and support to the concept by advocating a comprehensive vocational guidance plan for students (Miller, 1985).

Although the financial support of these programs has historically been assigned to general education, vocational educators have been strongly supportive of most, if not all, of them. One has only to look at their positive response to the career education initiative for proof. In many states, using state and local dollars and some flexible Federal research and development funds, vocational education funded the early awareness and exploration efforts, which were later subsumed under Federal career education funding. And for many years now, vocational guidance activities have been a legitimate expenditure of Federal, and in many cases, state vocational education funds.

In 1968, the National Advisory Council on Vocational Education said that an adequate system of vocational education should have the following characteristics:

1) Occupational preparation should begin in the elementary schools with a realistic picture of the world of work. Its fundamental purposes should be to familiarize the student with his world and to provide him with the intellectual tools and rational habits of thought to play a satisfying role in it.

2) In junior high school, economic orientation and occupational preparation should reach a more sophisticated stage with study by all students of the economic and industrial system by which goods and services are produced and distributed. The objective should be

exposure to the full range of occupational choices which will be available at a later point and full knowledge of the relative advantages and the requirements of each (Miller, 1985, 100).

The belief that students should be afforded the maximum opportunity for making informed career decisions is indigenous to vocational education. The support the field gives to initiatives that emphasize this approach provides ample evidence. It is difficult to understand this support, unless *most vocational educators believe:*

1) Occupational choice really is a process in the life of a person, not a singular event.
2) Vocational education has a vested interest in helping students make the best possible occupational choices for themselves.
3) Vocational education has a responsibility for helping students to develop decision-making skills.
4) Vocational education personnel can assist students in the decision-making process.
5) The instructional content of vocational education is valuable to the student in developing decision-making skills.
6) Vocational education has a more comprehensive purpose than just the teaching of specific job-entry skills.

Programmatic Separation or Integration

Early proponents of vocational education fought long and hard for the separation of its administration from that of general education and for its categorical funding. Critics (including the author) have long argued that this separatist attitude has resulted in vocational education becoming overly narrow, to the detriment not only of itself but to all of education (Leighbody, 1972).

Venn decried the ever-widening chasm that developed between the "traditionalists" and the "vocationalists" during the early part of the century. For in spite of the influence of persons such as Dewey on behalf of integrating vocational education into the general school program, the traditionalists refused to bend on what they considered to be academic essentials, and the vocationalists, in turn, were just as uncompromising in their demands for dramatic change. It should surprise no one that this failure to compromise left ". . . a heavy mark on the kind of vocational education which, inevitably, was put in the schools" (Venn, 1964, 51).

Venn went on to say that a narrow philosophy of vocational education grew out of these early conflicts, which was then spread throughout the schools of the land vis-à-vis the Smith-Hughes Act of 1917. He listed nine concepts that were embodied in this early philosophy, two of which were:

1) *Duality.* The historic antipathy of many general educators led the early vocationalists to believe that the integrity and success of a Federal program would depend on its administration by people familiar with and sympathetic to vocational education, and consequently the act's administrative provisions were so drawn as to encourage the separate administration of the program — the duality in the educational system which Dewey and others had so strongly opposed.

2) *Track.* Despite American abhorrence of European track systems, the practical and terminal provisions of the law meant that the student electing the vocational program after the ninth grade was severely limiting the chances for continuing his education beyond the high school.

On the other hand, Miller (1985) said that Prosser, in spite of his unequivocal commitment to a separately *administered* vocational education program, still believed that it should be a part of the public education system. Regardless, as reported earlier, Prosser established the initial tone of the administration of vocational education to keep it and general education as far apart as possible, so as not to contaminate ''real'' vocational education.

By the 1950s however, a broader perspective had begun to emerge. Conant's statement is an example of this different perspective, which was accepted by most vocational educators: ''Vocational education is not offered in lieu of general academic education, but it grows out of it, supplementing and enhancing it'' (Thompson, 1973, 113).

Somewhat later, Venn concluded that ''many of the assumptions underlying the existing structure of vocational education need reexamination in the light of the new relationship between man, his work, and education'' (1964, 66). And he and others thought they saw the light at the end of the tunnel when the Vocational Education Act of 1963 was enacted. This legislation seemed to sweep aside the years of division, isolation, confusion, resentment, and distrust and to offer an opportunity for the reexamination Venn called for. However, having the advantage of more years in which to review the results, Thompson (1973) argued that the 1963 Act actually did very little to increase the flexibility of vocational education.

In the 1970s, it became increasingly apparent that the future required moving toward a time when ". . . the dichotomy between so-called academic and vocational education is acknowledged to be outmoded, dysfunctional and extravagant" (Hammond, 1977, 109). Thompson had earlier said:

> . . . It is no longer possible to compartmentalize students for the purpose of assigning them to general, academic, and vocational components of education. Nor can education, itself, for that matter, be compartmentalized. We can talk about experiences that contribute to the individual's vocational education, but students are not to be rigidly assigned to it as a track. Education is a crucial element in all students' preparation for successful working careers. . . . Culture and vocation are inseparable and unseverable aspects of humanity. (1973, 225 – 226)

Just as the artificial distinctions of the past that separated vocational education from general and college preparatory education were a reflection of societal attitudes, so is the evolving perception, which seems to pay less attention to, if not do away with, some of these same distinctions. For example, sociologists are now saying that ". . . more and more people see work not as a separate activity but rather an integral part of the total life style" (Gottlieb, 1977, 41). Herein lies the hope for the demise of dualism, both outside and inside the school.

Venn (circa 1968) included the following statement in an article entitled, "A Message for School Administrators":

> . . . it would appear that the time has come for the "vocational" and "academic" to understand that the future will not tolerate either of us going it alone. The isolation of vocational education has hurt vocational education for a long time and is damaging the rest of education.

Most of those who have spoken in this section are not separatists. They do, however, see the need for maintaining the unique characteristics and integrity of vocational education. It is important to recognize that when a school or school system implements vocational education, it accepts an additional and specific responsibility that is different from and builds upon those of college preparatory and general education. This is the point that was missed by so many in 1917. While preparing persons for effective participation in an occupation or a group of occupations neither disparages nor eliminates the need for college preparatory or general education, it does extend those functions in important ways that, if not set aside but incorporated into the *persona* of the school, will change it completely and, for the most part, for the better.

So although many, if not most, vocational educators are concerned about separatism and wish to have no part of such an isolationist approach, they remain proud to be different enough to accomplish vocational education's different task. The emphasis for them, however, is on "different," not "separate."

All of this leads to the following inferences about what *most vocational educators believe:*

1) Vocational education is an integral part of the instructional program in comprehensive secondary and postsecondary institutions.

2) The different functions of general, college preparatory, and vocational education are complementary.

3) The strength of an education program is in providing different educational functions, not in making everything the same. Comprehensiveness is not synonymous with sameness.

4) Vocational education's function in a comprehensive education program remains sufficiently different to warrant categorical funding.

5) The disparity among vocational education, general education, and college preparatory education is not as severe as it once might have been.

6) The content of vocational education includes the same basic concepts as does that of college preparatory and general education.

7) The difference between vocational education and general and college preparatory education resides most in the methodologies used in the instructional process.

8) Vocational education should build upon the premises of and be integrated with general and college preparatory education.

9) The time is right to begin the integration of academic and vocational education.

Vocational Education and the Economy

The early advocates of vocational education left no doubt that they felt its primary purpose was economic, a consideration that continues to be important. As Thomas Johns, director of the Office of Vocational and Adult Education Analysis in the U.S. Department of Education, and one of his staff, Joyce A. Rice, recently wrote:

The original intent of the Congress in providing federal support for vocational education in 1917 was similar to current intent, to strengthen the nation's economic base through an efficient, well trained and productive workforce. (Personal correspondence, 1992)

Leighbody (1972, 29) reported that most vocational educators believe that if their program is offered:

1) The nation will be provided with the trained workers needed to maintain its economic health and growth.

2) Unemployment and underemployment caused by lack of training and education will be reduced or eliminated.

3) Many other social evils associated with unemployment and economic deprivation will be diminished.

4) Individuals will benefit by becoming productive and contributing members of society rather than its dependents, and many personal as well as social gains will result.

Evans said, "Obviously economics and occupational education are related in important ways" (1971, 95). And Thompson (1973, 18) was even more specific:

It is a generally held view that vocational education is to serve the economic system and thus, the labor market. This view is expressed in nearly every piece of literature that discusses economics and vocational education.

On the premise that vocational education can have a positive effect on the economy, Congress specified in Section 195 (5) (a) of the Educational Amendments of 1976:

. . . the State shall, in considering the approval of such applications [of local districts for vocational education funds], give priority to those applicants which—(i) are located in economically depressed areas and areas with high rates of unemployment . . . and (ii) which are new to the area served and which are designed to meet new and emerging manpower needs and job opportunities in the area and where relevant, in the State and the Nation.

In 1977, the *Yearbook of the American Vocational Association* was given over to the topic of vocational education and the nation's economy. Throughout this document, the implication was that there is a positive correlation between high quality vocational education and economic growth. During that same year, Levitan reiterated his belief that the rate of return from investing in people is much higher than that received from investing in machines, and, he added, ". . . vocational training pays off and is an essential component in any expanding economy" (1977, 61).

However, some interesting inconsistencies still exist:

> When really pushed on the point, few vocational educators believe that economic concern—the allocating policy of matching men and jobs—is the primary base of vocational education. They would more likely opt for a concern for the individual. (Thompson, 1973, 17—18)

Might it be that vocational education advocates, recognizing that its purported economic contributions make it quite attractive, particularly in times of economic difficulty, have oversold this function to the public and to the Congress? Some who have studied the situation closely argue that this may be the case. For example, Ginzberg argued that it is important to recognize that skill acquisition in the United States has multiple access points, and the difficulties young people have as they try to enter the world of work may have nothing to do with their preparation in school or, for that matter, in vocational education:

> The schools are not in a position, have never been in a position, and can't be in a position to create an adequate level of jobs. All they can do is prepare an adequate number of properly prepared youngsters. . . . In my view, we keep confusing problems of employability and employment. (Ginzberg, 1977, 24)

Vocational educators may even be somewhat naive, according to Gottlieb (1977), when they act as if enrolling in a good training program and possessing a positive work attitude are all that is required for persons to gain employment. He believed that there is a great deal of value in providing appropriate career learning experiences, but that there is more to the problem than just training.

So while many official statements about vocational education (e.g., legislation, rules, regulations, and policies) address its economic function, there is much evidence that its practitioners believe that this function, although important, is only one of several. All of this leads to the inferences that *most vocational educators believe:*

1) Education can produce new goods and services in the form of skills and techniques.

2) An individual's economic success is important to both the person and society.

3) Preparing individuals for participating in the marketplace is one of the purposes of education.

4) Vocational education is a form of education that is applicable to the economic needs of society.

5) There is a positive correlation between vocational education and economic growth.

6) Vocational education is responsible for the employability of a person.

7) Vocational educators are not totally responsible for the subsequent employment of persons they train.

8) Vocational education cannot eliminate unemployment.

SUMMARY

Each of the premises inferred in this chapter is a fragment of the philosophy of most vocational educators, undergirding and guiding their most successful practices. This compendium is a first step in building a comprehensive statement of educational philosophy. In truth, what has been done to this point is to develop a set of premises similar to the principles developed by Miller (1985), although somewhat more extensive.

The next step taken, in Chapter 10, is determining if these individual premises can be translated into the essential components of a comprehensive statement of educational philosophy.

The Philosophy of the Best of Vocational Education — Part 2

ORGANIZING THE PREMISES INTO A COMPREHENSIVE STATEMENT

TO determine if the premises inferred in Chapter 9 do, in fact, comprise a comprehensive statement (Part 2 of the inferential process), Frankena's (1966) model is adapted and used much like a philosophical template, allowing one to begin to organize the individual premises, identify the connections that exist between and among them, and judge the completeness of the tentative statement that emerges. This procedure is implemented on the following pages, following a more complete description and explanation of Frankena's work.

Each of the premises, as currently worded, will be placed in the section of the philosophical template that seems most appropriate (see Figure 10.1). This not only provides the necessary organization, but it also allows one to recognize the parent practice(s) from which the premise(s) originated and to track each premise into the final statement.

It is obviously within the prerogative of the reader to question the exact placement of the premises in the model. And it should be noted that some of the premises fall into more than one category, a phenomenon that does no violence to the model or the resulting statement. In fact, Frankena acknowledged that this was a possibility. In addition, the premises must still be edited for clarification and to reduce duplication and be rephrased into a more smoothly flowing statement.

The specifics of the resulting statement will not surprise most vocational educators, nor will their more academic counterparts find many new or unknown concepts. In fact, it is quite likely that both groups can accept most, if not all, aspects of it, but *that is precisely the point.*

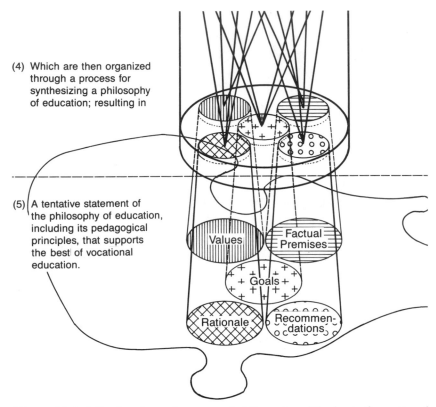

(4) Which are then organized
    through a process for
    synthesizing a philosophy
    of education; resulting in

(5) A tentative statement of
    the philosophy of education,
    including its pedagogical
    principles, that supports
    the best of vocational
    education.

Values

Factual Premises

Goals

Rationale

Recommen-dations

Figure 10.1 *Inferring the pedagogy and philosophy of the best of vocational education – Part 2.*

Beneath the surface, academic and vocational educators are, in fact, far more similar than they are different.

To reiterate an important point, this statement is still no more than a working version and a point of departure for additional deliberations. Its weaknesses include the subjective nature of the inferential process though which it was developed, the selectivity with which practices and documentation were chosen, its inclusion of author bias, the possibility that some premises have been inappropriately placed in the model as noted above, and its development through a somewhat drastic departure from more traditional and academic philosophic methods of inquiry. The author hopes that the field will take it sufficiently seriously to criticize and improve upon it. In so doing, they will sharpen their own analytical skills, and this tentative philosophy of education will be strengthened.

At a minimum, however, this exercise provides pedagogical and philo-sophical handles that one can use to grasp the essence of vocational education, historically an elusive task.

A CLOSER LOOK AT FRANKENA'S MODEL[3]

The main task of a philosophy is to state the dispositions to be fostered or cultivated, typically called its goals. But there must be a rationale that explains why the goals are desirable in the first place. Likewise, the thought pattern that specifies what should be done or how to reach those goals needs to be made explicit. Frankena (1966) proposed that, if completely worked out, a philosophy of education would include the following:

- a list of goals or objectives that the philosophy advocates [see Section C (p. 163)]
- a rationale (e.g., values and factual premises) upon which the goals are based [see Sections A and B (pp. 160 – 162)]
- recommendations about ways and means of organizing, teaching, and administering programs [see Section E (pp. 164 – 166)]
- a rationale (e.g., psychological, sociological, or pedagogical) upon which the recommendations are based [see Section D (pp. 163 – 164)]

The line of reasoning connecting these sections may take various forms, but all will constitute the same general pattern. They will start with some basic premises about that which is desirable or obligatory (Section A). However, one cannot infer from Section A to Section C (the goal statements) without some connecting premises such as those found in Section B; practice is always a combination of prescriptive convictions (Section A) and descriptive understanding (Section B). The remainder of the model is comprised of recommendations for reaching the goals proposed in Section C. These recommendations – the pedagogical strategies, including means, methods, curriculum, and administration – are made specific in Section E, while the reasons for making such recommendations appear in Section D.

[3]The author is indebted to Katy Greenwood (1978), whose work with the Frankena Model has shed much light upon the search for the philosophic roots of vocational education.

A TENTATIVE STATEMENT OF THE PHILOSOPHY OF EDUCATION THAT SUPPORTS THE BEST PRACTICES OF VOCATIONAL EDUCATION

Section A—Normative Statements of Value

1) Education is life, not preparation for life.
2) Meaningful learning experiences occur within the community of which the school is a part.
3) Each student is an important individual and must be treated with respect.
4) Students are responsible persons and should be treated as such.
5) Students are individuals who learn in different ways.
6) Vocational educators accept students in their current stage of maturity and help them grow from that point.
7) Students can make a contribution to their own learning experiences.
8) Students have the right and responsibility to participate in their own educational process, making some of the decisions concerning both themselves and that process along the way.
9) Students have the right to know their level of skill proficiency.
10) Education is responsible for providing students with statements of their level of achieved proficiency.
11) An individual's economic success is important to both the person and society.
12) As skills become more enterprise-specific, society's responsibility for providing such skills decreases.
13) The schools are not totally responsible for the education of their students; other societal institutions share in that responsibility.
14) The educational enterprise cannot and should not take full responsibility for helping students make the transition from school to work.

Section B—Premises Held to Be Factual

1) Vocational education is an integral part of the instructional program in comprehensive secondary and postsecondary institutions.

2) Vocational education has a more comprehensive purpose than just the teaching of specific job-entry skills.

3) The content of vocational education includes the same basic concepts as the content of college preparatory and general education.

4) The content of vocational education is more specific than that of general or college preparatory education.

5) Education can produce new goods and services in the form of skills and techniques.

6) Vocational education is a form of education that is applicable to the economic needs of society.

7) There is a positive correlation between vocational education and economic growth.

8) Vocational education is responsible for the employability of a person.

9) Vocational educators are not totally responsible for the subsequent employment of persons they train.

10) Vocational education cannot eliminate unemployment.

11) There is a career ladder within an occupational field, that runs from the semi-skilled to the technician and the professional.

12) Occupational choice really is a process in the life of a person, not a singular event.

13) Vocational education personnel can help students in the decision-making process.

14) The instructional content of vocational education is valuable to the student in developing decision-making skills.

15) Vocational education has a vested interest in students making the best possible occupational choices for themselves.

16) Workers will experience an increased need for retraining throughout their careers due to rapidly increasing technology and its effect upon their jobs.

17) The more technical the job requirements, the more need there is for the student to possess a conceptual understanding.

18) Basic academic skills are becoming increasingly important occupational competencies.

19) Students can be led through specific low-skill activities into the conceptual by skilled teachers as concepts are grasped.

20) Vocational education is a teaching/learning process that operates best in context-specific situations.

21) Vocational education, at its best, starts students in the specific and leads them into the conceptual (theoretical) abstraction as far as each is capable of going.

22) The student who develops conceptual skills can transfer those skills to new jobs as they emerge.

23) The more conceptual the nature of the skill, the more likely it is to be transferable.

24) Transferable skills are the most salable skills that vocational educators can help their students develop.

25) The strength of an education program is in providing different educational functions, not in making everything the same. Comprehensiveness is not synonymous with sameness.

26) Vocational education's function in a comprehensive education program remains sufficiently different to warrant categorical funding.

27) The different functions of general, college preparatory, and vocational education are complementary.

28) The disparity among vocational education, general education, and college preparatory education is not as severe as it once might have been.

29) The time is right to begin the integration of academic and vocational education.

30) The schools and their instructional program belong to the community.

31) The school is accountable to the community for the success of its program.

32) Community members have a responsibility to offer thoughtful and objective advice for improving vocational education programs.

33) Community members (individuals and institutions) want to become actively involved in schools and have much to offer all of education, particularly vocational education.

34) Vocational education teachers can secure valuable input from representatives of the community in instructional decisions.

Section C—Goals or Objectives the Philosophy Advocates

1) Preparing individuals for participating in the marketplace is one of the purposes of education.
2) Vocational education is responsible for providing students with specific job-entry skills.
3) The ultimate aim of vocational education is the learning of transferable conceptual skills.
4) Vocational education has a vested interest in helping students make the best possible occupational choices.
5) Vocational education has a responsibility for helping students develop decision-making skills.
6) One of the goals of vocational education is teaching students how to learn.
7) Vocational education is visibly applicable to the real world and can make the content of general education more relevant to the daily life of most students.

Section D—Empirical Evidence: Learning Theories, Research Base, Observations, and Experiences

1) The content of vocational education includes the same basic concepts as does that of college preparatory and general education.
2) The difference between vocational education and general and college preparatory education resides most in the methodologies used in the instructional process.
3) Vocational education instruction is experiential in nature.
4) Vocational education is a teaching/learning process that operates best in context-specific situations.
5) Students can be led through specific low-skill activities into the conceptual by skilled teachers as concepts are grasped.
6) Vocational education, at its best, starts students in the specific and leads them into the conceptual (theoretical) abstraction, as far as each is capable of going.
7) The most effective environment for learning is one that is as true-to-life as possible for the student.

8) The most effective teaching/learning situation is one that is a model of democracy in action.

9) Self-imposed goals for learning are more useful than goals imposed by others.

10) Many of the actions of students are reflections of teachers' expectations of them.

11) If students are given opportunities to exercise responsibility, they will respond accordingly.

12) Education is bound neither by geography nor time.

13) Students learn through all their experiences, not just those that occur in a classroom.

14) Using the workplace as a training site can be an important component of a skill development program.

15) The more specific the skill to be learned, the more appropriate the use of the actual job experience for training.

16) The use of the workplace as a training site should be coordinated by the teacher and take into account the needs of the student and the employer.

17) Careful planning on the part of the student, teacher, and employer should precede a student's cooperative work experience.

18) The placement and follow-up of students serves as one means of evaluating the effectiveness and integrity of vocational education instruction.

19) Although a placement service meets a vital need of students and their employers, its educational value is in its potential for redirecting instruction.

Section E—Recommendations about Ways and Means of Teaching

1) Vocational education instruction should be available to all citizens, youth and adults alike, at times they need it most.

2) The content of vocational education programs should have immediate and practical application to the world of work.

3) Vocational education content should be determined by an analysis of the competencies needed for success in the workplace.

4) Vocational education competencies should be identified by reviewing current job activities and making adjustments for predicted changes in the labor market.

5) Vocational education content should be arranged from the specific application to the general concept.

6) There is a great deal of commonality among jobs in the competencies that are required for success.

7) Vocational education programs should result in measurable outcomes that reflect the level of skill attained by each student.

8) The performance criteria used should be valid and reliable measures of competence.

9) The competencies to be taught and the criteria for success should be shared with the student at the beginning of the instructional experience.

10) Each student should practice the competency in question immediately and sufficiently to maximize the retention of what they are to learn.

11) Each student should be able to apply that which is being learned immediately.

12) Vocational education teachers should have subject matter mastery, including the specific skills, of the occupations in which they teach.

13) Many persons, in addition to baccalaureate-degreed teachers, are capable of providing instruction to students, and the necessary pedagogical training should be provided to experienced technicians, so they can perform as professional and competent teachers.

14) Vocational teachers can and should be evaluated on the skill levels attained by their students.

15) Vocational education can and should demonstrate its effectiveness through the process of competency testing.

16) Vocational education course content should be structured to provide exit and re-entry points for students, according to their needs and interests.

17) Vocational education should build upon the premises of and be integrated with general and college preparatory education.

18) Specific vocational education instruction should be provided as nearly as possible to the time when such instruction is applicable to the job needs of the individual.

19) Academic and vocational education subject matter should be integrated into a more holistic instructional program.

20) There should be a meshing or articulation of secondary and postsecondary vocational education curricula, so students can move easily from one level to the other.

21) The school's instructional program should complement the learning experiences that are available in the community, and all such experiences should be coordinated for the benefit of the student.

22) The school should open its doors to the citizens of its community, and in so doing, open the doors of the community to its students.

SUMMARY

If the objective of this exercise had been only to develop a philosophical statement to guide and promote the continued growth and development of vocational education, these premises would now be edited into just such a statement. However, this is not the case. Instead, the objective is to grasp the essence of the best of vocational education, which these premises provide, for inclusion in the pedagogical and philosophical core of tech prep. Therefore, the editing and rephrasing of these singular premises take place in the next chapter. The resulting statement addresses the larger context and venue of tech prep, rather than just vocational education.

However, the fact that such an editorial step is not taken at this point in no way limits the usefulness of this tentative statement for those who wish to understand vocational education better. In fact, this statement, including the specific premises as written, should be used by teams of academic and vocational education teachers as a starting point when they begin to develop their common pedagogy and philosophy. It is also recommended that they use the same or a similar inferential approach to refine these premises and identify the belief structure of the best of their academic practices. In this, as is the case in so much of educational reform and improvement, it may well be that the process through which these premises are derived is, ultimately, of most significance.

A Philosophical Point of Departure for Tech Prep

IF tech prep is more than vocational education, as has been claimed throughout this book, then the wording of its pedagogy and philosophy must be more comprehensive than the statement organized in Chapter 10. This is accomplished on the following pages by editing and revising words and phrases, as well as by deleting premises that speak only to or about vocational education and vocational educators, while taking a great deal of care to maintain the basic integrity of the original statement. If that integrity is not preserved, and if the resulting statement includes values, goals, or recommendations about ways and means of teaching that do not have their footings in specific practices, the value of the inferential process used thus far will be lost, and one might just as well develop a statement from thin air.

When this edited version is put in place (see Figure 11.1), while recognizing that *premises inferred from the most effective practices of academic education are still missing and must be added*, the construction of the conceptual foundation for tech prep (one of the objectives of this book) will near completion.

A PRELIMINARY STATEMENT OF PHILOSOPHY FOR TECH PREP

Section A—Normative Statements of Value

Education is life, not preparation for life. It is not limited to formal schooling. Instead, meaningful learning experiences occur within the entire community of which the school is a part.

167

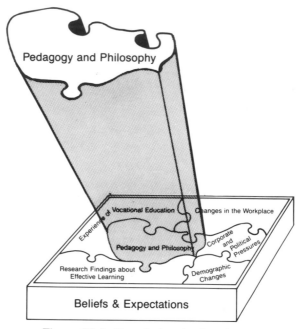

Figure 11.1 *Completing the foundation.*

Students are important and responsible individuals who have different learning styles. Educators should accept them as they are, and help them grow toward mutually acceptable goals. These students can make important contributions to their own learning, and have both the right and the responsibility to participate in their educational process, making some of the decisions about themselves and that process along the way.

All students have the right to know their level of proficiency and the progress they are making in the pursuit of agreed-upon goals. The educational institution in which they are enrolled is responsible for providing them with valid and reliable measures of that progress.

A person's successful economic activity is important to both the individual and society. However, society's responsibility for providing such skills decreases as the skills become more enterprise-specific. Nor are schools solely responsible for educating students, or for their subsequent transition from school to work. Instead, a partnership among education, other societal institutions, and the workplace is more effective in dealing with this increasingly important function.

Section B—Premises Held to Be Factual

Tech prep is an integral part of secondary and postsecondary instruction. However, its purpose is more comprehensive than just teaching specific job-entry skills. Its content includes the basic concepts of general and college preparatory education, which it presents in more specific and applied contexts.

Education influences the economy positively by producing new goods and services in the form of skills and techniques. Tech prep is especially responsive to changes in the marketplace, and is positively correlated with economic growth. However, although tech prep educators are responsible for the employability of their students, they are not responsible for their ultimate employment, which may be the result of many other mitigating factors. Tech prep cannot and will not eliminate unemployment.

There are career ladders running from the unskilled to the professional levels in most occupational fields. A student's decision about the proper career to pursue and which ladder(s) to climb is a process in which tech prep personnel and instructional content can make major contributions. Tech prep practitioners have a vested interest in their students making informed decisions and the best possible occupational choices.

Due to rapidly increasing technology and its effect upon their jobs, workers will experience an increased need for retraining throughout their careers. In particular, as technical jobs increase and approach levels previously held by professionals, more conceptual understanding will be needed by the workers, and basic academic skills will become increasingly important. The specific occupational skills included in most tech prep courses of study can be instructional stepping stones to these more conceptual skills.

Tech prep instruction embodies a context-specific learning process, which starts students in the specific skill or fact, and leads them through individualized instruction into the conceptual abstraction, as far as each is able to go. Students who attain deeper level conceptual skills will possess the more transferable and thus, the more salable, skills.

The comprehensiveness of an instructional program should not be confused with ''sameness.'' Although the function of tech prep in a comprehensive instructional program is different, it is still compatible with and complementary to the function of college prep and vocational education. The strength of administrators lies not in their treating everything the same, but in their ability to orchestrate different educational functions. Tech prep can, however, begin to eliminate the divisiveness of educational programs by integrating academic and vocational education instruction.

The schools and their instructional programs belong to the community of which they are a part, and the school is accountable to that community for its success. Conversely, community members have a responsibility to offer thoughtful and objective advice and assistance to improve their schools' instructional offerings. Many citizens want to become more actively involved in their schools and have much to offer. Educators are responsible for devising ways to secure and use this input on a regular and timely basis.

Section C—Goals or Objectives the Philosophy Advocates

The goals of technical preparatory education (grades 9 – 14) are to:

- provide students with information about the world of work as it is and as it should be
- help students develop decision-making skills
- help students learn how to learn
- prepare students to participate successfully in the marketplace, providing them with both specific job-entry skills and transferable, conceptual skills
- help educators reform secondary and postsecondary education by translating its instructional content into that which is relevant and applicable to the students' real world
- break down the artificial barriers between academic education and education for work.

Section D—Empirical Evidence: Learning Theories, Research Base, Observations, and Experiences

The content of tech prep programs of study and that of general and college preparatory education is the same. The differences reside most in the methodologies used in teaching and learning. Tech prep instruction is experiential and context-specific, and can move students from the specific fact or skill to the more abstract concept.

The best educational environment is one that is true-to-life for students, includes learning situations that are models of democratic action, and encourages students to set their own learning goals. Many of the actions of students are reflections of the teachers' expectations of them, and if they are given an opportunity to exercise responsibility, students will respond accordingly.

Education is bound neither by geography nor time; students learn through all their experiences, including those outside the classroom. The actual job site is particularly appropriate for teaching and learning a specific job skill. However, its use as a training site requires careful planning and coordination, taking into account the needs of both the student and the employer.

One of the measures of the effectiveness of tech prep is the degree to which students who complete the programs of study secure employment in the career cluster for which they have been educated. Placement and follow-up activities help determine the consistency of the instructional offerings with the needs of society, and can be used to redirect that instruction, if necessary.

Section E—Recommendations about Ways and Means of Teaching

Tech prep, or instruction based upon similar pedagogical concepts, should be available to all citizens when they need it most. The content of such instruction should be determined by an analysis of the workplace, and have immediate and practical application therein. This should be accomplished by reviewing current practices in job clusters, and adjusting for predicted changes in the labor market. To facilitate learning, instructional content should be arranged and presented from the specific application to the general concept. Many jobs require the same broad-based competencies, which should be provided in all appropriate programs of study.

Tech prep programs of study should result in measurable outcomes that validly and reliably reflect the levels of skill attained by each student. The competencies to be mastered and the criteria for mastery should be shared with the students at the beginning of the instructional process. Each student should practice the competency immediately and sufficiently to maximize its retention, and be able to apply what they learn without delay.

Tech prep teachers and faculty should possess the technical and pedagogical competencies necessary to prepare their students for success in their career cluster. In some cases, competent technicians, in addition to baccalaureate-degreed teachers, should be given the necessary training and used as professional faculty. The effectiveness of tech prep teachers and faculty, as well as the initiative itself, should be evaluated through an assessment of the competencies gained by the students and their eventual placement in the job market.

Tech prep programs of study should provide flexible exit and re-entry points for students, and should integrate the concepts and skills of academic and vocational education into a more holistic instructional format. Secondary and postsecondary portions of these programs of study should be connected to facilitate students moving easily from one to the other, and instruction in enterprise-specific skills, if offered at all, should be provided as nearly as possible to the time when students will use such instruction.

Tech prep programs of study should complement the learning experiences that are available in the community, and all such experiences should be coordinated for the benefit of the student. Tech prep should help the school open its doors to its community, and in so doing, open the doors of the community to its students, thereby fostering a partnership in the educational process.

Building upon the Foundation

THE first three purposes of this book, as stated on page 2, were to:

1) Identify the current strengths and weaknesses of tech prep.
2) Explore the relationship between tech prep and vocational education, and identify the contributions vocational education can make to tech prep and *vice versa*.
3) Build a conceptual foundation upon which practitioners can construct their own, more effective, tech prep initiatives.

The construction of the conceptual foundation for tech prep has now been completed (see Figure 12.1). Standing upon this foundation, practitioners can see more clearly, and comprehend more completely the complexities that confront them as they build their tech prep initiatives. Local tech prep planners are encouraged to use the components of this conceptual foundation as building blocks in the construction of their own approach.

And by going beyond the information presented in this book and seeking answers to pertinent questions about their local situation, practitioners can conceptualize strategies that are not only consistent with this paradigm, but, more importantly, fit the specific needs of their community. They can make more intelligent decisions about adopting or adapting elements from models that exist in other communities. And if those who have already implemented tech prep in their school, school district, and postsecondary institution perceive that aspects of their current initiative are not as effective as they should be, they can use this foundation as a basis for understanding their dilemma better and responding accordingly.

Tech prep *can* make a major contribution to the reform of secondary and postsecondary education, if it is conceptualized as one of many quality improvement processes, and if it is incorporated into a com-

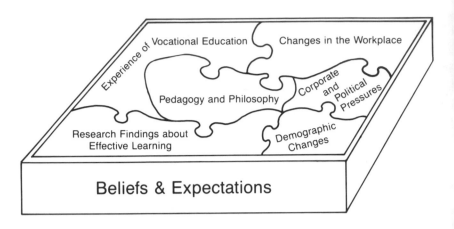

Figure 12.1 *The complete foundation.*

prehensive, long-range plan for systemic change that is led by top-level system administrators. It *can* serve as a vital force in the integration of academic and vocational education, thus beginning to reduce the dualism that has existed in American public education almost from the beginning. It *can* make the content of education more relevant to the day-to-day life and needs of the majority of American students, and provide a clear pathway for them from early adolescence into the evolving labor market of the twenty-first century.

On the other hand, if it is narrowly construed, tech prep's contributions will not only be less beneficial, but, in some instances, it may actually get in the way of progressive and necessary educational reform. It was pointed out early in Chapter 1 that three pitfalls loom in the path of the successful implementation of tech prep as a long-term, comprehensive educational reform strategy:

1) The assumption that any specific programmatic configuration of tech prep is the goal, rather than a means to a more important end
2) The lack of a conceptual understanding of tech prep to guide its design, implementation, and evaluation as an educational reform process or strategy and its subsequent connection with other educational reform efforts
3) The failure to recognize that the massive systemic change required of the educational establishment will not occur, no matter how effective the tech prep initiative may be, without external support

The preceding chapters have, for the most part, addressed pitfalls one and two on the premise that they must be dealt with first. The reader should now be better able to negotiate both of these, and begin to deal with the third in a more effective fashion.

It was also hypothesized that educational practitioners would be more likely to build the desired comprehensive initiatives, if they had a clear conceptual understanding of tech prep. And if they could see how that understanding was developed and how its various components fit together into a conceptual foundation, they would be able to conceptualize approaches that are more consistent with their unique situations.

The conceptual foundation that has been developed includes consumers' beliefs about and expectations of their schools, the changing demographic characteristics of consumer populations, characteristics of the changing world of work, the influence of the corporate and political sectors, the latest research findings about how people learn best, the experience of vocational education, and, at its core, a pedagogy and educational philosophy to guide and direct tech prep as a context-specific and experiential mode of instruction. As that foundation was built, the practitioner was given guidance and direction, at almost every step, for adjusting the national dimensions of the component under consideration to the special characteristics of the local situation.

The relationship of tech prep and vocational education has, without a doubt, received the most attention in these pages. This has been done without apology—an effective tech prep initiative must be built upon the lessons learned (oftentimes, the hard way) by vocational education over the past seventy-five years, and it will include the essence of vocational education—the pedagogy and philosophy that undergirds the best and most effective of its practices. Although the belief structure that supports general and college preparatory education must also be included at the heart of tech prep, this book began with vocational education and thereby, provided a process for those who, hopefully, will now analyze other more academic instructional approaches in a similar manner.

Purposes 4 and 5 of this book were to:

4) Identify the consistencies that exist between tech prep, total quality management, and total quality education.
5) Connect tech prep with total quality education (TQE), and show how tech prep, in conjunction with TQE, can help the school, school district, and postsecondary institution make long-term sys-

temic change and continuously improve the quality of the product and service provided its consumers.

It has been shown that a comprehensive view of tech prep allows and, in fact, demands that it be incorporated into holistic educational reform, which, hopefully, is increasing at the local level. There is no jarring dysfunction experienced when connecting tech prep with total quality management and total quality education. In fact, they are consistent in many ways. In addition, a planning process is provided in Chapter 13, which, if followed, will place a system's tech prep initiative right at the heart of its larger reform effort, whether called total quality management, total quality education, or by some other name.

Total Quality Management, Total Quality Education, and Tech Prep: Making Connections

OF all the educational reform initiatives to burst upon the scene in recent years, none has caught the imagination of more persons nor offered as much hope for dealing with the real problems of education as has total quality education (TQE). Those who are the least bit familiar with TQE recognize it as an adaptation of the work of W. Edwards Deming (1986), whose ". . . name is suddenly everywhere" (Bonstingl, 1992, 4). In fact, Deming's status is approaching that of legend, with his having been credited with almost single-handedly providing the Japanese the management tools that brought them from the depths of economic and industrial despair at the end of World War II to their present position in the international marketplace. And he is now turning his attention to American business, industry, *and* education.

However, Deming may be somewhat dismayed and even displeased by the familiarity with which some toss his name and catchy phrases like "total quality" around these days, especially in education. The problem is not that his work does not have relevance; indeed, it is completely relevant. The problem is the simplistic view that some are taking of the application of his concepts to education, looking to TQE as an end, rather than as a means to a larger end. A reading of his work clearly displays his belief that the concept of total quality, although a worthwhile goal, is not a state to be reached or a stage to be mounted. Instead, *the emphasis is on the continuous improvement of quality, focusing on the process of making improvements more than on the improvements themselves*. Once again, the temptation is to expect too much too soon, casting a shadow upon the potential effectiveness of this reform process. Those who are in the educational reform game only for the short run will get little from TQM or TQE (or tech prep, for that matter), and will contribute even less to the improvement of education.

177

WHAT IS TOTAL QUALITY MANAGEMENT (TQM)?

In his book, *Out of the Crisis*, Deming (1986) enunciates and elaborates upon his now-famous Fourteen Points or principles for transformation. They are:

1) *Create constancy of purpose for improvement of product and service.* Of the two types of problems faced by an organization — problems of today and problems of tomorrow — the latter demand the most attention. Solving long-term problems requires constancy of purpose, which, in turn, demands that the organization accept the obligation to innovate, put resources into research and education, and constantly strive to improve the design of its product and service. This improvement ". . . never ceases," and "the consumer is the most important ingredient in the production process" (Deming, in process).

2) *Adopt the new philosophy.* The importance of this step, which almost sounds trite, or most assuredly, redundant, cannot be overlooked or underestimated. What Deming means is, don't just give lip-service to it, do it. This kind of commitment to change must eventually be embraced by all the members of an organization. However, it must begin at the top, and top management must constantly reinforce this new way of thinking through their *actions* as well as their words. There is no such thing as being halfway pregnant with the concept of continuous improvement of quality; you either are or are not committed. And everyone in the organization, from the lowest on the totem pole to the highest, will know exactly where top management stands.

3) *Cease dependency on mass inspection.* Deming compares routine 100 percent inspections designed to improve quality with admitting that you don't believe your own process can meet your own goals or, in his words, ". . . planning for defects" (Deming, 1986, 28). It is also a strategy that is too late to do any good and much too costly. Once the product reaches the inspection point, its quality is already fixed. "Quality comes not from inspection, but from improvement of the production process" (Deming, 1986, 29). (What does this say about the current "politically correct" high school exit exam idea?)

4) *End the practice of awarding business on the basis of price tag*

alone. Deming warns that short-term gain, such as that which might be secured through low-bid purchasing, can, in the long run, be the most expensive for an organization. Instead of seeking the cheapest price for an item, the "aim in purchase of tools and other equipment should be to minimize the net cost [over time]" (Deming, 1986, 32). But this requires long-term thinking and measures of quality of the item or service being purchased. Deming stresses the advantages of developing a long-term relationship with a single source of supply, building and maintaining a high level of *trust and mutual confidence* between the purchaser and vendor. This leads to a dedication of all the employees of a firm and its suppliers to competitive excellence by minimizing waste in every form.

5) *Improve constantly and forever the system of production and service*. Quality must be improved at every step in the production process, from design to delivery, changing the focus from meeting arbitrary specifications to seeking greater uniformity in product and service, ". . . working for less and less variation about [a] nominal value" (Deming, 1986, 49).

6) *Institute training*. Deming believes that "the greatest waste in America is failure to use the abilities of people" (1986, 53). Training has to become a way of life for all employees, from top executives to new workers. And such training must take into account the different learning styles of the trainers.

7) *Adopt and institute leadership*. Leadership and supervision are not synonymous. Management must work continuously on improving the process and translating their intent and commitment to improve quality into both the design of the product (or service), as well as the actual product (or service) itself.

> Leaders must know the work they supervise. They must be empowered and directed to inform upper management concerning conditions that need correcting. . . . [And] management must act on the corrections proposed. (Deming, 1986, 54)

Perhaps, most surprising to many, Deming advocates completely doing away with a focus on outcomes, such as those promoted by management by numbers, management by objectives, work standards, meeting specifications, zero defects, and personal performance appraisals.

8) *Drive out fear*. Managing through fear simply doesn't work. The

most productive workplaces are those in which ideas can be expressed freely and without fear of reprisal. Commitment to continuous quality improvement requires an attitude of openness and honesty on the part of all workers, an attitude achieved only when the workers are sufficiently secure to be honest with themselves, their peers, and their leaders.

9) *Break down barriers between staff areas.* The more of an entire process employees see and understand, the more likely they are to recognize their place and importance in and to that process. They will also be empowered to make appropriate suggestions for improving the performance of the task, which benefits the entire process. The more ownership an individual employee has of the entire process, the more interest in and commitment to the process and the organization he/she will feel, and subsequently act out.

10) *Eliminate slogans, exhortations, and targets for the work force.* These methods just don't work. About all they do is create work for those who design and print them. Who among the workforce is likely to do a better job simply because of a slogan put on a wall or on a company letterhead? Not many, nor are they likely to respond to motivational techniques that seem manipulative. No one likes to be, or even feel as if they are being, manipulated. On the other hand, goals and targets that are intrinsically established by those who have to meet them are a different matter. Again, the focus is on internal, rather than external, motivation.

11) *Eliminate numerical quotas for both the workforce and management.* Calling such quotas a burlesque, Deming says:

> A natural fluctuation in the right direction is interpreted as success. A fluctuation in the opposite direction sends everyone scurrying for explanations and into bold forays whose only achievements are more frustration and more problems. (1986, 75)

12) *Remove barriers that rob people of pride of workmanship.* Return to the worker that which is his/her birthright: "The right to be proud of their work, the right to do a good job" (Deming, 1986, 77). Quit treating people like a commodity. Management must learn how to face and deal with *people* problems, rather than hoping they will go away if ignored.

13) *Encourage education and self-improvement for everyone.* An organization needs more than just good people. It needs people who

are willing to improve themselves with education, and it needs to provide these people with the necessary educational opportunities. However, the workers themselves must generate much of the interest in self-improvement. ''One should not wait for promise of reimbursement [to enroll in] a course of study'' (Deming, 1986, 86).

14) *Take action to accomplish the transformation.* Top management must struggle with and adopt the thirteen points above and agree on their meaning, the direction to take, and how to carry out the new philosophy. They must take pride in their new philosophy and in breaking with tradition. They must explain the new philosophy and approach to a critical mass of people in the company to make sure that a sufficient number understand these principles and what they mean to them and to the organization. Lastly, every activity and every job in the company must be seen as a stage upon which the improvement process is carried out—there are *no* unimportant acts or actors.

WHAT IS TOTAL QUALITY EDUCATION (TQE)?

Total quality management (TQM) offers very real and practical assistance to those who are struggling to reform education. To begin with, being grounded as it is in a systemic approach to continuous improvement, it promises to end the isolation of educators from one another and the community of which they are a part; requiring instead the full participation of all those who have an interest in the educational process. It recognizes that the system, not individuals (students, teachers, and administrators), is most responsible for educational results. This recognition takes away the need to blame anyone, and releases the energy that normally goes into defensive actions to deal with real problems. Beyond that, total quality education provides a new set of tools to educators, which they can use to discover and correct flaws in the system (Savary, 1992, 1–2).

When the concept of continuous quality improvement becomes a way of life in a school or a school system, good things usually begin to happen (Savary, 1992). The application of Deming's principles to education is not particularly difficult, because the concepts upon which he bases his approach are not foreign to much of American education. The difference is that TQM and thus, TQE, *demand that top management exert leadership over the entire system through a holistic approach to improving quality*, rather than through the piecemeal approaches that have swamped educational practitioners since the early 1960s.

Some of the most obvious consistencies between the concepts of TQM and educational reform include their common emphasis upon the following (Savary, 1992, 3):

- meeting and exceeding the needs of the consumers or customers of the educational process (a customer being any recipient of a product or service from others inside or outside the system)
- working for continuous, rather than stop-gap improvement
- collaborating with other agencies to get the job done (not worrying about who gets credit)
- identifying common and special causes of variation
- considering and managing organizations (in this case, schools) as systems
- recognizing that problems fundamentally stem from the system and its processes, not its workers (students, teachers, and administrators)
- working in teams
- investing in employee education and training
- believing that people want to do well and will take responsibility, when they see a purpose for their work

Bonstingl (1992) translated Deming's Fourteen Points into what he calls the Four Pillars of total quality management, which are particularly applicable to education:

1) *The organization must focus, first and foremost, on its suppliers and customers.* In a TQM organization, everyone plays both roles at one time or the other, and understanding the systemic nature of the work in which one is involved requires understanding these dual roles.

2) *Everyone in the organization must be dedicated to continuous improvement, personally and collectively.* Bonstingl advocates schools becoming "learning organizations in which people, processes, and systems are dedicated to continuous learning [by] and improvement [of]" the teachers, administrators, and other staff, as well as the students (1992, 6).

3) *The organization must be viewed as a system, and the work people do within the system must be seen as an ongoing process.* While not completely letting students and teachers off the hook, Bonstingl points out that they are less to blame for educational failure than is the system. He quotes Deming and others as suggesting that ". . . more than 85 percent of all the things that go wrong in any organization are directly attributable to how the organization's system and processes are set up" (1992, 7).

4) *The success of total quality management is the responsibility of top management.* Without concerted, visible, and constant dedication by those at the top to incorporating quality improvement principles and practices as part of the deep culture of the organization, failure is assured (1992, 6−7).

This approach will become a whole new way of life for those who implement it, and will affect them outside school as well as on their daily jobs. Isolation among the workers (teachers) and between workers and management (administrators) will be ended. But training will be essential, and all those who are involved need to recognize that they have not chosen an easy pathway to success (Bonstingl, 1992).

Kaufman and Hirumi warn against an overly simplistic adaptation of TQM to education, saying that "a satisfied customer is not enough; a continuously healthy, safe, and well-served customer is better" (1992, 33). They suggest ten steps to move to what they call "Total Quality Management Plus" in education (1992, 34):

1) Be ready for a challenge. Understand that people fear change and that education is comprised of people. Proceed with courage, patience, and understanding.

2) Create and use a quality system that will collect performance data, and share with the TQM partners so everyone can clearly and continuously determine strategies and tactics for improvement.

3) Define the ideal vision, the world in which we want our grandchildren to live. Identify results only, do not include processes, resources, or methods.

4) Determine gaps between current results and the ideal vision.

5) Based on the ideal vision, obtain agreement on what would deliver client satisfaction next year, five years from now, and into the next century. Agree on how satisfaction will be measured.

6) Identify results that would demonstrate achievement of steps three and four, and describe how you would measure each. These results might be mastery in courses, skills, knowledge, attitudes, and/or abilities.

7) Define the activities that would deliver such results.

8) Identify resources—including people, facilities, and funds—that are required to do the activities and deliver the required results.

9) Specify what each person must do and accomplish to make certain that quality results and activities happen continuously.

10) Continue to use the data-based quality system, which objectively and accurately tracks and reports progress, problems, and opportunities. The educational system should be revised as required, and new opportunities to improve elements of the system should be considered at each step. Improvement should occur steadily without sacrificing successful activities and resources.

TECH PREP AND TOTAL QUALITY EDUCATION (TQE)

When properly conceptualized, tech prep shows the following consistencies with TQE that allow its incorporation in and major contribution to the change process:

1) TQE focuses on improving education through reforming its processes; tech prep itself is an educational reform process.

2) TQE demands that the entire system be included in the improvement of quality; tech prep is a holistic and systemic approach to quality improvement.

3) TQE requires the involvement and commitment of all the workers in an organization; tech prep promotes maximum ownership of the initiative by all its participants.

4) Both TQE and tech prep are built on a dynamic theory of change.

5) Both require that top management have a clear vision of that change, including its short-term costs and long-range benefits to the organization and its consumers.

6) TQE requires top-level leadership and commitment; tech prep must be led by the school principal, district superintendent, and postsecondary institution president.

7) Both are driven by consumer satisfaction with their product or service.

8) Both use objective data for constant monitoring and improvement of the process, as well as the product or service.

9) TQE requires that all participants continue to educate themselves; tech prep motivates students to learn and encourages them to become lifelong learners.

10) Both are built upon a belief in the innate ability and integrity of the organization's personnel.

11) Both require a heavy investment in the continuing education, training, and staff development of these personnel.

12) Both promote and are totally dependent upon teamwork, and developing a high level of trust among those who participate.

At least one potential inconsistency between the two has already been noted – the possibility that tech prep might focus on competency-based or outcome-based assessment to the point that such measures become numerical specifications of excellence. This need not happen, if practitioners are aware of the potential problem, and, instead, use such measures as general outcomes of significance as suggested.

A PLANNING PROCESS FOR DEVELOPING A TECH PREP INITIATIVE AS A PART OF TQE

The planning process that follows (see Figure 13.1) is built upon these consistencies and can be used to incorporate tech prep into on-going TQE reform initiatives. Although this planning process is designed for a consortium of school districts and a cooperating postsecondary institution (the most common tech prep configuration), it can be used by a single school, school district, or community college to institute educational reform. If no comprehensive reform initiative exists, this planning process should be used to initiate continuous quality improvement throughout the system, beginning with tech prep.

Task One

Top management (district superintendent[s] and cooperating postsecondary institution president) should, in concert, identify the critical problems facing their institutions, communities, and service area.

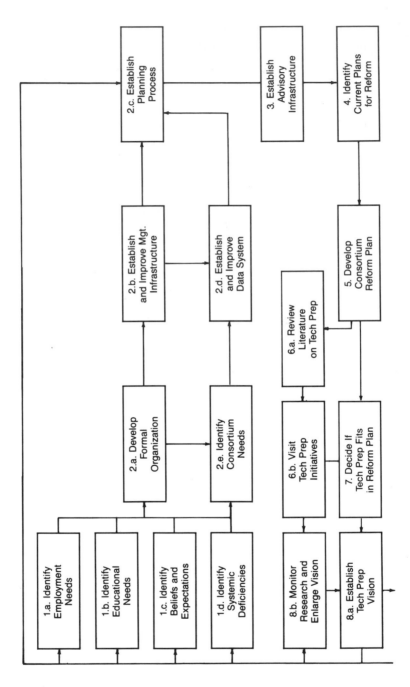

Figure 13.1. A process for planning and implementing a comprehensive tech prep educational reform strategy, using the principles of TQM and TQE.

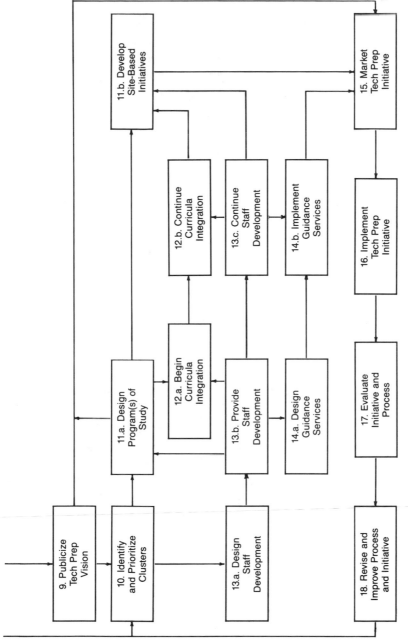

Figure 13.1 (continued).

187

a) Develop and maintain a clear picture of the present and future employment needs (local, regional, national, and international) and opportunities.

b) Identify the short-term and long-range educational needs of the populations served by the member institutions.

c) Identify the beliefs and expectations of the consumers of the member institutions' products and services.

d) Identify the systemic deficiencies of the participating educational institutions in meeting consumers' expectations.

Task Two

Top management should establish, empower, and maintain a formal organization or consortium, charging it with creating a single system and using the collaborative action of its individual members to address the problems identified in Task One.

a) Develop and enter into a public, written agreement to collaborate on identifying and dealing with common problems.

b) Establish and empower a management infrastructure to plan and oversee any collaborative activities undertaken by the consortium.

c) Design and adopt a planning process that addresses the identified needs of the consortium, and is responsive to the system's consumers at every step in the change process.

d) Establish and maintain a central data system in which is stored and from which is disseminated local, regional, national, and international labor market information, pertinent demographics, educational data, and consumer expectations and reactions for use by the consortium leadership in making decisions about how to improve the quality of the system's (consortium's) products and services for its consumers.

e) Identify other needs of the consortium that are precipitated by the charge and responsibilities it has been given, as they emerge.

Task Three

Authorize, establish, and maintain a representative advisory infrastructure to provide input from consumers at all levels and stages of the change process.

Task Four

Identify plans that currently exist in the cooperating members' organizations to deal with the problems identified in Task One.

a) Identify all the educational reform activities currently taking place in the consortium region, from the kindergarten through the post-secondary levels.
b) Identify and become familiar with other reform initiatives in the community (e.g., corporate and governmental).
c) Identify the changes that are anticipated because of these activities.
d) Identify the theoretical premises (e.g., market responsiveness, pedagogy, economic development, community involvement, citizen empowerment, improved governmental efficiency, etc.) upon which these activities are built.

Task Five

Share these plans among the cooperating partners and consolidate or synthesize into a consortium-wide approach in which all have ownership. If certain consortium members have no such plans, encourage them to use this initiative to generate one.

Task Six

Become knowledgeable about tech prep. Review all the information that is available, study (and visit, if necessary) some of the more established models, and secure input from as many successful practitioners as possible, making sure to learn about problems as well as potential.

Task Seven

Decide if tech prep can fit into the consortium members' plan for long-term educational change and, if so, how it will fit. *This must be a conscious decision by top management, and their only legitimate reason for initiating tech prep is the belief that it can contribute to the goals the group has already established for reforming education in its member institutions and the service area.*

Task Eight

If the answer is in the affirmative; conceptualize, establish, maintain, and continually revise a vision of tech prep as a strategy for responding to the consortium's identified needs. Identify the theoretical and conceptual connections that exist between tech prep and the other organizational reform strategies already in place in the region.

Task Nine

Top management should immediately identify and recognize tech prep as a major educational reform strategy they plan to implement, show where it fits in their long-range plans for comprehensive change, and begin the on-going process of demonstrating their commitment to this strategy to all participants and the general public.

Publicize the tech prep vision, focusing initially on prospective consumers (students, their teachers and parents, and potential employers). This is a first step in marketing the initiative.

Task Ten

Identify the cluster area(s) upon which the consortium will focus its initiative.

a) Review the labor market data collected in Task One a) very carefully (get outside professional assistance, if necessary). Look for both entry-level opportunities and career ladders upon which students may climb.

b) Review the educational information available from all the consortium's member institutions, including student aspiration and career guidance data.

c) Prioritize the clusters, based upon the projected employment needs and the institutional capability of the system's members to begin a specific initiative. (With regard to the latter point, begin with a cluster for which many of the instructional elements are already in place, although they may need to be rearranged. In other words, set yourself up for success, not failure.)

Task Eleven

Design and implement a clearly defined four- or six-year program of study for each of the cluster areas chosen.

a) Identify and appoint a consortium-wide curriculum committee comprised of employers from the job cluster chosen and teachers (secondary and postsecondary; academic, vocational, and technical) who will provide the instruction.

b) Identify the competencies (both academic and technical) needed for success on the job in the chosen cluster. Use the results of any DACUM processes that may have been conducted earlier, and get all available competency-based instructional material from your respective state department of education or one of the curricula consortia that specialize in such materials (e.g., V-TECS, MECC, and NOCTI).

c) Arrange the competencies into a continuum, from the simple and specific to the complex and more theoretical.

d) Determine the level and sites at which these competencies will be taught, recognizing that many of them may need to be introduced early and reinforced often and that secondary sites may differ in their approaches.

e) Identify competency measures that all the instructional staff (secondary and postsecondary; academic, vocational, and technical) agree reflect acceptable performance and will be considered to be valid and reliable by all the consortium's member institutions.

f) Compare the continuum with the secondary and postsecondary instruction currently being offered in the member institutions, identifying and filling any instructional gaps and deleting any overlaps that may exist.

g) Add applied academic courses, as they are needed and appropriate.

h) Produce and distribute descriptive literature, that makes the purposes of the curricular pathway and the pathway itself clear to students, their parents, teachers, and potential employers. Work closely on this step with guidance and counseling personnel, as well as with marketing staff members.

Task Twelve

Integrate the academic and technical instructional content in the program(s) of study at both the secondary and postsecondary sites. (See Chapter 14 for specific suggestions for implementing this task.)

Task Thirteen

Provide the staff development necessary for all participants to carry out the planned activities, at critical times dictated by implementation of other tasks.

Task Fourteen

Provide comprehensive career guidance services at the secondary and postsecondary levels, so students can make more intelligent choices about career goals, select appropriate educational experiences, and reach those goals.

Task Fifteen

Develop and implement a public information and marketing program that focuses initially on specific consumers (students, parents, and potential employers).

Task Sixteen

Implement the initiative.

Task Seventeen

Evaluate the initiative through formative and summative evaluation techniques, focusing primarily on the process and determining ways to improve it. Conduct placement and follow-up activities of the students who matriculate through the programs of study to determine if the content is (and remains) appropriate for the task. Revise as necessary.

Task Eighteen

Improve the tech prep initiative *and* the planning and implementation process through continuous review, monitoring, evaluation, and revision.

SUMMARY

The consistencies between total quality management, total quality education, and a comprehensively conceived tech prep initiative are clear. The task of educational administrators, their policy making boards, and, most importantly, their faculties and staff will be much less difficult as they set off down the road of educational reform, if they combine the concepts of these major educational improvement strategies.

An Introduction to Integrating Academic and Vocational Education

IT has been stressed from the very beginning that, for a tech prep initiative to be effective, the best of vocational education and the best of academic (general and college preparatory) education must be integrated into a holistic program of study. It has also been made clear that this is a complex task, and that it requires those most intimately involved (teams of academic and vocational teachers) to develop a common pedagogy and philosophical base upon which they can meet before they can put together their different methodologies. This chapter provides guidance and direction to those who wish to establish, lead, and implement such a process.

APPROACHES TO INTEGRATING ACADEMIC AND VOCATIONAL EDUCATION

Grubb (1991, 11−52) identified eight models for integrating academic and vocational education, all of which currently exist in America's schools:

- incorporating academic content in vocational courses
- linking academic and vocational teachers to enhance academic competencies in vocational courses
- making the academic curriculum vocationally relevant
- curricular alignment, modifying both academic and vocational courses
- the senior project as a form of integration
- the academy
- occupational high schools and magnet schools
- occupational clusters, career paths, and occupational majors

Each of these methods has its own peculiarities, as well as its unique strengths and weaknesses. For example, while incorporating academic content into vocational courses is the simplest form of integration, it requires no collaboration among teachers, the integrated academic skills are typically remedial, and it has not proven to be very effective in most cases. Likewise, efforts that focus on making the academic curriculum vocationally relevant, while letting the vocational programs remain intact (applied academics are common examples of this approach), leave the integration process primarily up to academic teachers, and do not themselves promote cross-curricular collaboration.

The model that appears to offer the most hope for success in a comprehensive tech prep initiative is curricular alignment. This approach modifies both academic and vocational courses, and integration occurs at the program of study level, rather than at the individual course level. Both academic and vocational courses are modified and linked. Academic courses incorporate more occupationally relevant material, and vocational courses incorporate more academic or basic instruction. In addition, the content of the academic and vocational instruction is coordinated, with horizontal alignment taking place when students learn about similar subjects at the same time in both their academic and vocational classes, and vertical alignment taking place when students take academic and vocational courses sequentially.

Other advantages of the curricular alignment model include:

1) Currently employed academic and vocational teachers collaborate to modify courses; there is no need to hire additional personnel.

2) Academic and vocational courses already in place in the curriculum are modified to integrate the instructional program; new courses need not be added.

However, all is not a bed of roses, even in this approach. For example, academic and vocational teachers must receive a great deal of training and staff development and work constantly to ensure that their instructional content is consistent and mutually reinforcing. This takes a lot of time. And, due to the uniqueness of each locality and the individual teachers in that locality, curricula must be developed locally; purchasing materials off the shelf is almost impossible.

INTEGRATING CURRICULA AT A LOCAL SITE

Whereas many of the activities conducted through a comprehensive tech prep initiative are implemented consortium-wide, *the integration of instruction is always site specific*, no matter which of the models is chosen. Therefore, the steps proposed below should take place at each participating site. Since they are an elaboration of Tasks Eleven b) and Twelve in the planning process, several assumptions are made about earlier tasks in that process having been completed before beginning this activity:

1) Top administrative officers at the school, school district, and postsecondary institution level will have identified tech prep as a major educational reform strategy and will be giving it their continuous support and direction.

2) The system's vision of tech prep will identify its centerpiece as a focused, articulated, and *integrated* program(s) of study.

3) The employment cluster(s) to which the program(s) of study provides a pathway for students will have been identified and prioritized.

4) A specific program of study will have been developed that includes the responsibilities of and plans for each specific site (secondary school, postsecondary institution, or apprenticeship program) collaborating in that program of study.

5) The competencies (academic, vocational, and technical) required for success in the selected cluster(s) will have been identified through a valid and reliable process (e.g., DACUM, V-TECs, MECC, or NOCTI), a continuum of these competencies will have been constructed (from simple to complex), and valid and reliable competency test items will have been identified and agreed upon by all concerned parties.

6) Arrangements will have been made for appropriate staff development to be available to the teachers and administrators to whom the task of integrating instruction will be assigned.

If these assumptions are correct:

1) Appoint a curriculum integration team at each site. This team should include key academic and vocational or technical teachers at the site whose collective instructional areas, including applied academics, and expertise encompass the competencies to be taught, a guidance counselor, and the principal (or, if this is impossible, the assistant principal for instruction).

Keep the number of team members relatively small and manageable (probably no more than ten). Choose persons who are excited about the prospect of integrating instruction, who will devote the necessary time and energy to the task (volunteers may be better), and who will truly represent their instructional peers. Give the team members the time necessary to complete the task (both hours and days, in the short run, and years to make lasting changes).

2) Provide the team with the necessary staff development. This should include an introduction to the concept of tech prep as an educational reform strategy, the latest research on how people learn best, information about the experience (successful and unsuccessful) of the SREB curricula integration sites (visit them, if possible) and the sites identified by the National Center for Research in Vocational Education, recent work of the National Council of Teachers of Mathematics (NCTM), and instruction in cooperative learning, outcome-based education (OBE) and other cutting-edge reform strategies.

3) All other faculty members and staff at the site should be made completely aware of the integration initiative, its purposes, and the fact that the ultimate goal is to spread this instructional process through the entire school. Keeping other faculty members and staff apprised of both the successes and failures of the team is imperative—this has to be an open process.

4) Team members should identify and make a commitment to a common pedagogy and educational philosophy upon which they will build their integrated activities. This may require outside consultant assistance. A first step, however, for those who wish to initiate the process, involves having the team members begin to go through the exercise provided in Appendix B.

5) Team members should compare the portion of the competency continuum for which they are responsible with the instructional content currently being provided at the site, identifying possible gaps and redundancies in that instruction.

6) Team members should identify those competencies that are subject-specific (e.g., math, communications, or business) and those that cross instructional lines. The team members should not attempt to integrate all of their instruction content. Instead, they should agree upon a few carefully selected cross-curricula competencies upon which they will initially focus their attention and efforts.

7) The team members should be broken down into sub-groups to begin their integration activities, always reporting back to the larger group. For example, two teachers might attempt to integrate Biology and Health Occupations I, while others work on Mathematics and Physics, or Communications and Business. It would be ideal, at this point, to involve any applied academic teachers and their course material as core players and components.

8) Each sub-group should plan a segment of instruction, identifying the competencies to be taught through the integrated activities, the complementary activities that will be undertaken in the separate classes, the different and reinforcing methodologies that will be used, and the measures for assuring competency mastery.

9) Each sub-group should implement the planned activities, conduct an immediate evaluation, and provide feedback to all team members. Don't be surprised if everything doesn't go right the first time. Remember, all this is new to everybody. The most important thing is not to quit, just keep improving the process.

10) Once team members are comfortable with integrating two instructional areas, they may begin to put three, four, and even more together. The important thing is to keep making corrections and build upon the team members' success.

11) The entire process must be led by the principal (or designee) and monitored, critiqued, and evaluated on a continuous basis, apprising all other faculty and staff members in the school of the progress being made by the team and gradually bringing them into the process.

12) Staff development should continue to be provided to team members, and, increasingly, to all faculty and staff.

Some Concluding Thoughts

IF local tech prep practitioners choose to use the tools provided them in this book and wherever else they may find concepts of comparable comprehensiveness, then tech prep can begin to make the contributions dreamed of by many. If, on the other hand, they insist on wrapping it into a neat package, which admittedly may assist them in handling it for the moment, and then become more enamored of the package than the concepts it contains, tech prep, like so many of its predecessors, will last for a time and then fade from the scene.

Even if tech prep comes to an unfortunate and untimely demise, one thing is sure: American education will continue its march down the path away from the traditional book-centered curriculum of the past, which truly serves no one well, toward more context-specific, experiential instructional approaches that are much more consistent with the way people really learn. It would be a shame if tech prep took itself out of this parade, for it stands on the threshold of leading a major breakthrough into that more effective type of instructional experience. A great deal hangs in the balance.

State Data Center Program Coordinating Organizations

Alabama

Center for Business and
  Economic Research
University of Alabama
Box 870221
Tuscaloosa, AL 35487-0221
*Ms. Annette Watters
(205) 348-6191

Alabama Department of
  Economic and Community
  Affairs
Office of State Planning
P.O. Box 250347
3465 Norman Bridge Road
Montgomery, AL 36125-0347
Mr. Parker Collins
(205) 284-8630

Alabama Public Library Service
6030 Monticello Drive
Montgomery, AL 36130

Ms. Hilda Dent
(205) 277-7330

Alaska

Alaska State Data Center
Research & Analysis
Department of Labor
P.O. Box 25504
Juneau, AK 99802-5504
*Ms. Kathryn Lizik
(907) 465-4500

Office of Management and
  Budget
Division of Policy
Pouch AD
Juneau, AK 99811
Mr. Jack Kreinheder
(907) 465-3568

Department of Education
Division of Libraries and
  Museums

Includes Business and Industry Data Center Initiative Components. List compiled by
United States Department of Commerce, Bureau of the Census, Washington, D.C.,
October, 1992.
  *Denotes key contact SDC.
**Denotes key contact BIDC.

Alaska State Library
Pouch G
Juneau, AK 99811
Ms. Catherine Gruenberg
(907) 465-2927

Department of Community &
  Regional Affairs
Division of Municipal &
  Regional Assistance
P.O. Box BH
Juneau, AK 99811
Ms. Laura Walters
(907) 465-4756

Institute for Social & Economic
  Research
University of Alaska
3211 Providence Drive
Anchorage, AK 99508
Mr. Jim Kerr
(907) 786-7710

Arizona (BIDC)

DES 045Z
First Floor, Southeast Wing
1789 West Jefferson St.
Phoenix, AZ 85007
*,**Ms. Betty Jeffries
(602) 542-5984

Center for Business Research
College of Business
  Administration
Arizona State University
Tempe, AZ 85287
Mr. Tom Rex
(602) 965-3961

College of Business
  Administration
Northern Arizona University
Box 15066
Flagstaff, AZ 86011
Dr. Joseph Walka
(602) 523-3657

Federal Documents Section
Department of Library,
  Archives, and Public Records
1700 West Washington, 2nd
  Floor
Phoenix, AZ 85007
Ms. Janet Fisher
(602) 542-4121

Division of Economic &
  Business Research
College of Business & Public
  Administration
University of Arizona
Tucson, AZ 85721
Ms. Holly Penix
(602) 621-2155

Arkansas

State Data Center
University of Arkansas-Little
  Rock
2801 South University
Little Rock, AR 72204
*Ms. Sarah Breshears
(501) 569-8530

Arkansas State Library
1 Capitol Mall
Little Rock, AR 72201

Ms. Mary Honeycutt
(501) 682-2864

Research & Analysis Section
Arkansas Employment Security
    Division
P.O. Box 2981
Little Rock, AR 72203
Mr. Coy Cozart
(501) 682-3159

California

State Census Data Center
Department of Finance
915 L Street
Sacramento, CA 95814
*Ms. Linda Gage, Director
(916) 322-4651
Mr. Richard Lovelady
(916) 323-2201

Sacramento Area COG
106 K Street, Suite 200
Sacramento, CA 95814
Mr. Bob Faseler
(916) 441-5930

Association of Bay Area
    Governments
Metro Center
8th and Oak Streets
P.O. Box 2050
Oakland, CA 94604-2050
Ms. Patricia Perry
(510) 464-7937

Southern California
    Association of Governments

818 West 7th Street, 12th Floor
Los Angeles, CA 90017
Mr. Javier Minjares
(213) 236-1800

San Diego Association of
    Governments
First Federal Plaza
401 B Street, Suite 800
San Diego, CA 92101
Ms. Karen Lamphere
(619) 236-5353

State Data Center Program
University of California-
    Berkeley
2538 Channing Way
Berkeley, CA 94720
Ms. Ilona Einowski/Fred Gey
(510) 642-6571

Association of Monterey Bay
    Area Governments
445 Reservation Road
P.O. Box 838
Marina, CA 93933
Mr. Frank Barron
(408) 883-3750

Colorado

Division of Local Government
Colorado Department of Local
    Affairs
1313 Sherman Street, Room
    521
Denver, CO 80203
*Mr. Reid Reynolds
Ms. Rebecca Picaso
(303) 866-2156

Business Research Division
Graduate School of Business
    Administration
University of Colorado-Boulder
Boulder, CO 80309
Richard Wobbekind
(303) 492-8227

Natural Resources &
    Economics
Department of Agriculture
Colorado State University
Fort Collins, CO 80523
Ms. Sue Anderson
(303) 491-5706

Documents Department
The Libraries
Colorado State University
Fort Collins, CO 80523
Ms. Suzanne Taylor
(303) 491-1880

Connecticut (BIDC)

Policy Development and
    Planning Division
Connecticut Office of Policy
    and Management
80 Washington Street
Hartford, CT 06106-4459
*,**Mr. Bill Kraynak
(203) 566-8285

Government Documents
Connecticut State Library
231 Capitol Avenue
Hartford, CT 06106

Mr. Albert Palko
(203) 566-4971

Roper Center
Institute for Social Injury
University of Connecticut
U-164
Storrs, CT 06269-1164
Ms. Lois Timms-Ferrara
(203) 486-4440

Connecticut Department of
    Economic Development
865 Brook Street
Rocky Hill, CT 06067-3405
Mr. Jeff Blodgett
(203) 258-4239

Employment Security Division
Connecticut Department of
    Labor
200 Folly Brook Boulevard
Wethersfield, CT 06109
Mr. Richard Vannuccini
(203) 566-2120

Delaware (BIDC)

Delaware Development Office
99 Kings Highway
P.O. Box 1401
Dover, DE 19903
*,**Ms. Judy McKinney-
    Cherry
(302) 739-4271

College of Urban Affairs and
    Public Policy
University of Delaware

Graham Hall, Room 286
Academy Street
Newark, DE 19716
Mr. Ed Ratledge
(302) 451-8406

District of Columbia

Data Service Division
Mayor's Office of Planning
Room 570, Presidential Bldg.
415 12th Street, N.W.
Washington, DC 20004
*Mr. Gan Ahuja
(202) 727-6533

Metropolitan Washington
    Council of Governments
777 North Capitol St., Suite 300
Washington, DC 20002-4201
Mr. Robert Griffiths
Ms. Jenean Johanningmeier
(202) 962-3200

Florida (BIDC)

Florida State Data Center
Executive Office of the
    Governor
Office of Planning & Budgeting
The Capitol
Tallahassee, FL 32399-0001
*Mr. Steve Kimble
(904) 487-2814

Center for the Study of
    Population
Institute for Social Research
654 Bellemy Building

Florida State University
Tallahassee, FL 32306-4063
Dr. Ike Eberstein
(904) 644-1762

State Library of Florida
R. A. Gray Building
Tallahassee, FL 32399-0250
Ms. Lisa Close
(904) 487-2651

Bureau of Economic Analysis
Florida Department of
    Commerce
107 East Gaines Street
315 Collins Building
Tallahassee, FL 32399-2000
**Ms. Amy Schmeling
(904) 487-2971

Georgia

Division of Demographic &
    Statistical Services
Georgia Office of Planning and
    Budget
254 Washington Street, S.W.
Room 640
Atlanta, GA 30334
*Ms. Marty Sik
(404) 656-0911

Documents Librarian
Georgia State University
University Plaza
Atlanta, GA 30303
Ms. Gayle Christian
(404) 651-2185

Robert W. Woodruff Library
  for Advanced Studies
Emory University
Atlanta, GA 30322
Ms. Elizabeth McBride
(404) 727-6880

Main Library
University of Georgia
Athens, GA 30602
Ms. Susan C. Field
(404) 542-0664

Georgia Department of
  Community Affairs
Office of Coordinated Planning
100 Peachtree St., N.E. #1200
Atlanta, GA 30303
Mr. Phil Thiel
(404) 656-5526

Documents Librarian
State Data Center Program
Albany State College
504 College Drive
Albany, GA 31705
Ms. Juanita Miller
(912) 430-4799

Documents Librarian
State Data Center Program
Georgia Southern College
Statesboro, GA 30460
Ms. Lynn Walshak
(912) 681-5117

State Data Center Program
Mercer University Law Library

Mercer University
Macon, GA 31207
Mr. Ismael Gullon
(912) 752-2668

Data Services
University of Georgia Libraries
6th Floor
Athens, GA 30602
Ms. Hortense Bates
(404) 542-0727

Prince Gilbert Memorial
  Library
Georgia Institute of Technology
Atlanta, GA 30332
Mr. Richard Leacy
(404) 894-4519

Guam

Guam Department of
  Commerce
590 South Marine Drive
Suite 601, 6th Floor GITC
  Building
Tamuning, Guam 96911
*Mr. Peter R. Barcinas
(671) 646-5841

Hawaii

Hawaii State Data Center
Department of Business &
  Economic Development &
  Tourism
220 S. King Street, Suite 400
Honolulu, HI 96813
(mailing address)

P.O. Box 2359
Honolulu, III 96804
*Ms. Jan Nakamoto
(808) 586-2493

Information and
   Communication Services
   Division
State Department of Budget and
   Finance
Kalanimoku Building
1151 Punchbowl Street
Honolulu, HI 96813
Ms. Joy Toyama
(808) 548-6180

Idaho

Idaho Department of Commerce
700 West State Street
Boise, ID 83720
*Mr. Alan Porter
(208) 334-2470

Institutional Research
Room 319, Business Building
Boise State University
Boise, ID 83725
Mr. Don Canning
(208) 385-1613

The Idaho State Library
325 West State Street
Boise, ID 83702
Ms. Stephanie Nichols
(208) 334-2150

Center for Business Research
   and Services

Campus Box 8450
Idaho State University
Pocatello, ID 83209
Dr. Paul Zelus
(208) 236-2504

Illinois

Division of Planning and
   Financial Analysis
Illinois Bureau of the Budget
William Stratton Building,
   Room 605
Springfield, IL 62706
*Ms. Suzanne Ebetsch
(217) 782-1381

Census & Data Users Services
Department 4690
Research Service Building,
   Suite A
Illinois State University
Normal, IL 61761-6901
Dr. Roy Treadway/Dr. Del
   Ervin
(309) 438-5946

Center for Governmental
   Studies
Northern Illinois University
Social Science Research Bldg.
DeKalb, IL 60115
Ms. Ruth Anne Tobias
(815) 753-1901, ×221

Chicago Area Geographic
   Information Study
Department of Geography,
   M/C 092

P.O. Box 4348
University of Illinois at Chicago
Chicago, IL 60680
Mr. Jim Bash
(312) 996-6367

Northeastern Illinois Planning
    Commission
Research Services
400 West Madison Street
Chicago, IL 60606-2642
Max Dieber/Mary Cele Smith
(312) 454-0400

Indiana (BIDC)

Indiana State Library
Indiana State Data Center
140 North Senate Avenue
Indianapolis, IN 46204
Mr. Ray Ewick, Director
*Ms. Roberta Eads
(317) 232-3733

Indiana Business Research
    Center
Indiana University
10th and Fee Lane
Bloomington, IN 47405
Dr. Morton Marcus
(812) 855-5507

Indiana Business Research
    Center
801 West Michigan, B.S. 4015
Indianapolis, IN 46202-5151
**Ms. Carol Rogers
(317) 274-2205

Research Division
Indiana Department of
    Commerce
1 North Capitol, Suite 700
Indianapolis, IN 46204
Mr. Robert Lain
(317) 232-8959

Iowa

State Library of Iowa
East 12th and Grand
Des Moines, IA 50319
*Ms. Beth Henning
(515) 281-4350

Census Services
Iowa State University
320 East Hall
Ames, IA 50011
Dr. Willis Goudy
(515) 294-8337

Center for Social and
    Behavioral Research
University of Northern Iowa
Cedar Falls, IA 50614
Dr. Robert Kramer
(319) 273-2105

Iowa Social Science Institute
University of Iowa
345 Shaeffer Hall
Iowa City, IA 52242
Mr. Brian Dalziel
(319) 335-2371

Census Data Center
Department of Education

Grimes State Office Building
Des Moines, IA 50319
Mr. Steve Boal
(515) 281-4730

Research Section
Iowa Department of Economic
    Development
200 East Grand Avenue
Des Moines, IA 50309
(515) 281-3005

Kansas

Division of the Budget
Room 152-E
State Capitol Building
Topeka, KS 66612
Ms. Teresa Floerchinger
(913) 296-0025

State Library
Room 343-N State Capitol
    Building
Topeka, KS 66612
*Mr. Marc Galbraith
(913) 296-3296

Institute for Public Policy and
    Business Research
607 Blake Hall
The University of Kansas
Lawrence, KS 66045-2960
Ms. Thelma Helyar
(913) 864-3123

Center for Economic
    Development & Business
    Research

Box 48
Wichita State University
Wichita, KS 67208
Ms. Janet Nickel
(316) 689-3225

Population and Resources
    Laboratory
Department of Sociology
Kansas State University
Manhattan, KS 66506
Dr. Jan L. Flora
(913) 532-5984

Kentucky (BIDC)

Center for Urban & Economic
    Research
College of Urban & Public
    Affairs
University of Louisville
Lousville, KY 40292
*,**Mr. Ron Crouch
(502) 588-7990

Office of Policy & Management
State of Kentucky
Capitol Annex
Frankfort, KY 40601
Mr. Steve Rowland
(502) 564-7300

State Library Division
Department for Libraries &
    Archives
300 Coffeetree Road
P.O. Box 537
Frankfort, KY 40601

Ms. Brenda Fuller
(502) 875-7000

Louisiana

Office of Planning and Budget
Division of Administration
P.O. Box 94095
1051 N. 3rd Street
Baton Rouge, LA 70804
*Ms. Karen Paterson
(504) 342-7410

Division of Business and
  Economic Research
University of New Orleans
Lake Front
New Orleans, LA 70148
Mr. Vincent Maruggi
(504) 286-6980

Division of Business Research
Louisiana Tech University
P.O. Box 10318
Ruston, LA 71272
Dr. Edward O'Boyle
(318) 257-3701

Reference Department
Louisiana State Library
P.O. Box 131
Baton Rouge, LA 70821
Mrs. Blanche Cretini
(504) 342-4918

Center for Life Cycle and
  Population Studies
Department of Sociology
Room 126, Stubbs Hall

Louisiana State University
Baton Rouge, LA 70803-5411
Mr. Pete McCool, Director
(504) 388-5359

Center for Business and
  Economic Research
Northeast Louisiana University
Monroe, LA 71209
Dr. Jerry Wall
(318) 342-1215

Maine

Division of Economic Analysis
  and Research
Maine Department of Labor
20 Union Street
Augusta, ME 04330
Mr. Raynold Fongemie,
  Director
*Ms. Jean Martin
(207) 289-2271

Maine State Library
State House Station 64
Augusta, ME 04333
Mr. Gary Nichols
(207) 289-5600

Maryland (BIDC)

Maryland Department of State
  Planning
301 West Preston Street
Baltimore, MD 21201
*,**Mr. Robert Dadd
Ms. Jane Traynham
(410) 225-4450

Computer Science Center
University of Maryland
College Park, MD 20742
Mr. John McNary
(301) 405-3037

Government Reference Service
Pratt Library
400 Cathedral Street
Baltimore, MD 21201
Mr. Wesley Wilson
(410) 396-5468

Small Business Development
   Center
217 E. Redwood Street, 9th Fl
Baltimore, MD 21202
Mr. Eliot Rittenhouse
(410) 333-6995

Massachusetts (BIDC)

Massachusetts Institute for
   Social and Economic
   Research
128 Thompson Hall
University of Massachusetts
Amherst, MA 01003
*,**Dr. Stephen Coelen,
   Director
(413) 545-3460
Ms. Nora Groves
(413) 545-0176

Massachusetts Institute for
   Social and Economic
   Research
Box 219
The State House, Room 50

Boston, MA 02133
Mr. William Murray
(617) 727-4537

Michigan

Michigan Information Center
   Department of Management
   & Budget
Office of Revenue and Tax
   Analysis
P.O. Box 30026
Lansing, MI 48909
*Mr. Eric Swanson
(517) 373-7910

MIMIC/Center for Urban
   Studies
Wayne State University
Faculty/Administration Bldg.
656 W. Kirby
Detroit, MI 48202
Dr. Mark Neithercut/Kurt
   Metzger
(313) 577-8350

The Library of Michigan
Government Documents Service
P.O. Box 30007
Lansing, MI 48909
Ms. F. Anne Diamond
(517) 373-1307

Minnesota (BIDC)

State Demographer's Office
Minnesota Planning
300 Centennial Office Building
658 Cedar Street
St. Paul, MN 55155

*Mr. David Birkholz
(612) 296-2557
**Mr. David Rademacher
(612) 297-3255

Metropolitan Council Data
  Center
230 E. 5th Street
St. Paul, MN 55101
(612) 291-8140

Interagency Resource &
  Information Center
Department of Education
501 Capitol Square Building
St. Paul, MN 55101
Ms. Patricia Tupper
(612) 296-6684

Mississippi (BIDC)

Center for Population Studies
The University of Mississippi
Bondurant Bldg., Room 3W
University, MS 38677
Dr. Max Williams, Director
*Ms. Rachel McNeely,
  Manager
(601) 232-7288

Governor's Office of Federal-
  State Programs
Department of Community
  Development
301 West Pearl Street
Jackson, MS 39203-3096
Mr. Jim Catt
(601) 949-2219

Division of Research and
  Information Systems
Department of Economic and

Community Development
1200 Walter Sillas Building
P.O. Box 849
Jackson, MS 39205
**Mr. Bill Rigby
(601) 359-2674

Missouri (BIDC)

Missouri State Library
600 W. Main Street
P.O. Box 387
Jefferson City, MO 65102
*Ms. Kate Graf
(314) 751-1823

Missouri Small Business
  Development Centers
300 University Place
Columbia, MO 65211
**Max E. Summers
(314) 882-0344

Office of Administration
124 Capitol Building
P.O. Box 809
Jefferson City, MO 65102
Mr. Ryan Burson
(314) 751-2345

Office of Computing
University of Missouri-St.
  Louis
8001 Natural Bridge Road
St. Louis, MO 63121
Dr. John Blodgett
(314) 553-6014

Office of Social & Economic
  Data Analysis

University of Missouri-
  Columbia
224 Lewis Hall
Columbia, MO 65211
Ms. Evelyn J. Cleveland
(314) 882-7396

Geographic Resources Center
University of Missouri-
  Columbia
4 Stewart Hall
Columbia, MO 65211
Dr. Christopher Salter

Montana (BIDC)

Census and Economic
  Information Center
Montana Department of
  Commerce
1424 9th Avenue
Helena, MT 59620
*,**Ms. Patricia Roberts
(406) 444-4393

Montana State Library
1515 East 6th Avenue
Capitol Station
Helena, MT 59620
Ms. Kathy Brown
(406) 444-3004

Bureau of Business and
  Economic Research
University of Montana
Missoula, MT 59812
Mr. Jim Sylvester
(406) 243-5113
Survey Research Center
Wilson Hall, Room 1-108

Montana State University
Bozeman, MT 59717
Ms. Lee Faulkner
(406) 994-4481

Research & Analysis Bureau
Employment Policy Division
Montana Department of Labor
  & Industry
P.O. Box 1728
Helena, MT 59624
Cathy Shenkle
(406) 444-2430

Nebraska

Center for Applied Urban
  Research
The University of
  Nebraska-Omaha
Peter Kiewit Conference Center
1313 Farnam-on-the-Mall
Omaha, NE 68182
*Mr. Jerome Deichert
Tim Himberger
(402) 595-2311

Policy Research Office
P.O. Box 94601
State Capitol, Room 1319
Lincoln, NE 68509-4601
Ms. Prem L. Bansal
(402) 471-2414

Federal Documentation
  Librarian
Nebraska Library Commission
1420 P Street
Lincoln, NE 68508-1683
(402) 471-2045

Nebraska Department of Labor
550 South 16th Street
P.O. Box 94600
Lincoln, NE 68509-4600
Mr. Robert H. Shanahan
(402) 471-2518

The Central Data Processing
   Division
Department of Administration
   Services
1312 State Capitol
P.O. Box 95045
Lincoln, NE 68509-5045
Mr. Skip Miller
(402) 471-4862

Natural Resources Commission
301 Centennial Mall South
P.O. Box 94876
Lincoln, NE 68509-4876
Mr. Mahendra Bansal
(402) 471-2081

Nevada

Nevada State Library
Capitol Complex
401 North Carson
Carson City, NV 89710
Ms. Joan Kerschner
*Ms. Betty McNeal
(702) 687-5160

New Hampshire

Office of State Planning
2 1/2 Beacon Street
Concord, NH 03301

*Mr. Tom Duffy
(603) 271-2155

New Hampshire State Library
20 Park Street
Concord, NH 03301-6303
Mr. John McCormick
(603) 271-2239

Office of Biometrics
University of New Hamphire
Pettee Hall
Durham, NH 03824
Mr. Owen Durgin
(603) 862-1700

New Jersey (BIDC)

New Jersey Department of
   Labor
Division of Labor Market and
   Demographic Research
CN 388-John Fitch Plaza
Trenton, NJ 08625-0388
*,**Ms. Connie O. Hughes,
Asst. Dir.
(609) 984-2593

New Jersey State Library
185 West State Street
CN 520
Trenton, NJ 08625-0520
Ms. Beverly Railsback
(609) 292-6220

CIT—Information Service
Princeton University
87 Prospect Avenue
Princeton, NJ 08544

Ms. Judith S. Rowe
(609) 258-6052

Center for Computer &
  Information Services
Rutgers University
CCIS-Hill Center, Busch
  Campus
P.O. Box 879
Piscataway, NJ 08854
Ms. Mary Jane Face Cedar
(908) 932-2889

Rutgers University — The State
  University
Kilmer Campus
Lucy Stone Hall, B Wing
New Brunswick, NJ 08903
Dr. James Hughes, Chair and
  Graduate Director
(908) 932-3822

New Mexico (BIDC)

Economic Development and
  Tourism Department
1100 St. Francis Drive
Santa Fe, NM 87503
Ms. Maritza Brown
(505) 827-0300

New Mexico State Library
325 Don Gaspar Avenue
P.O. Box 1629
Santa Fe, NM 87503
Ms. Laura Chaney
(505) 827-3826
Bureau of Business and
  Economic Research

University of New Mexico
1920 Lomas NE
Albuquerque, NM 87131
*Mr. Kevin Kargacin
(505) 277-6626
**(505) 277-2216

Department of Economics
New Mexico State University
Box 30001
Las Cruces, NM 88003
Dr. Kathleen Brook
(505) 646-4905

New York (BIDC)

Division of Policy Research
Department of Economic
  Development
1 Commerce Plaza, Room 905
99 Washington Avenue
Albany, NY 12245
*,**Mr. Robert Scardamalia
(518) 474-1141

Cornell University
CISER Data Archive
262 Caldwell Hall
Ithaca, NY 14853
Ms. Ann Gray
(607) 255-4801

New York State Library
Cultural Education Center
Empire State Plaza
Albany, NY 12230
Ms. Mary Redmond
(518) 474-3940
Nelson A. Rockefeller Institute
  of Government

411 State Street
Albany, NY 12203
(518) 472-1300

Division of Equalization and
  Assessment
16 Sheridan Avenue
Albany, NY 12210
Mr. Wilfred B. Pauquette
(518) 474-6742

North Carolina (BIDC)

North Carolina Office of State
  Planning
116 West Jones Street
Raleigh, NC 27603-8005
*,**Ms. Francine Stephenson,
Director of State Data Center
(919) 733-4131

State Library
North Carolina Department of
  Cultural Resources State
  Library
109 East Jones Street
Raleigh, NC 27611
Mr. Joel Sigmon
(919) 733-3270

Institute for Research in Social
  Science
University of North Carolina
Manning Hall CB 3355
Chapel Hill, NC 27599-3355
Mr. Glenn Deane
(919) 966-3346

Land Resources Information
  Service
Division of Land Resources
P.O. Box 27687
Raleigh, NC 27611
Ms. Karen Siderelis/Tim
  Johnson
(919) 733-2090

North Dakota

Department of Agricultural
  Economics
North Dakota State University
Morrill Hall, Room 224
P.O. Box 5636
Fargo, ND 58105
*Dr. Richard Rathge
(701) 237-8621

Office of Intergovernmental
  Assistance
State Capitol, 14th Floor
Bismarck, ND 58505
Mr. Jim Boyd
(701) 224-2094

Department of Geography
University of North Dakota
Grand Forks, ND 58202
Mohammad Hemmasi
(701) 777-4246

North Dakota State Library
Liberty Memorial Building
Capitol Grounds
Bismarck, ND 58505
Ms. Susan Pahlmeyer
(701) 224-2490

Ohio

Ohio Data Users Center
Ohio Department of
    Development
P.O. Box 1001
Columbus, OH 43266-0101
*Mr. Barry Bennett
(614) 466-2115

State Library of Ohio
65 South Front Street
Columbus, OH 43215
Mr. Clyde Hordusky
(614) 644-7051

Cleveland State University
Northern Ohio Data and
    Information Service
Euclid Avenue and East 24th
    Street
Cleveland, OH 44115
Mr. Mark Salling
(216) 687-2209

Ohio State University
    Library/Census Data Center
126 Main Library
1858 Neil Avenue Mall
Columbus, OH 43210
Marge Murfin
(614) 292-6175

University of Cincinnati
Southwest Ohio Regional Data
    Center
Institute for Policy Research
Mail Loc. 132

Cincinnati, OH 45221
(513) 556-5082

Oklahoma (BIDC)

Oklahoma State Data Center
Oklahoma Department of
    Commerce
6601 Broadway Extension
(Mailing address)
P.O. Box 26980
Oklahoma City, OK 73126-0980
*,**Jeff Wallace
(405) 841-5184

Oklahoma Department of
    Libraries
200 N.E. 18th Street
Oklahoma City, OK 73105
Mr. Steve Beleu
(405) 521-2502

Oregon

Center for Population Research
    and Census
Portland State University
P.O. Box 751
Portland, OR 97207-0751
Mr. Ed Shafer
*Ms. Maria Wilson-Figueroa
(503) 725-5159

Oregon State Library
State Library Building
Salem, OR 97310
Mr. Craig Smith
(503) 378-4276

Bureau of Governmental
Research & Service
University of Oregon
Hendricks Hall, Room 331
1408 University St.
P.O. Box 3177
Eugene, OR 97403
Ms. Karen Seidel
(503) 346-5235

Oregon Housing Agency
1600 State Street, Suite 100
Salem, OR 97310-0161
Mr. Mike Murphy
(503) 373-1611

State Service Center for
Geographic Information
Systems
Department of Energy Bldg.
625 Marion Street NE
Salem, OR 97310
Mr. Kenneth C. Yingling
(503) 378-4040

Pennsylvania (BIDC)

Pennsylvania State Data Center
Institute of State and Regional
Affairs
Pennsylvania State University
at Harrisburg
Middletown, PA 17057-4898
*,**Mr. Michael Behney
(717) 948-6336

Pennsylvania State Library
Forum Building
Harrisburg, PA 17105

Mr. John Gerswindt
(717) 787-2327

Penn State at Harrisburg
Acquisitions
Heindel Library
Middletown, PA 17057-4898
Ms. Grace M. Finn
(717) 948-6074

Puerto Rico

Puerto Rico Planning Board
Minillas Government Center
North Bldg., Avenida De Diego
P.O. Box 41119
San Juan, PR 00940-9985
*Sra. Lillian Torres Aguirre
(809) 728-4430

Recinto Universitario De
Mayaguez
Edificio Anexo Pineiro
Carretera Num 2
Mayaguez, PR 00708
Prfa. Grace Quinones Seda
(809) 834-4040

Biblioteca Carnegie
Ave. Ponce De Leon-Parada 1
San Juan, PR 00901
Sra. Carmen Martinez
(809) 724-1046

Rhode Island

Department of Administration
Office of Municipal Affairs
One Capitol Hill
Providence, RI 02908-5873

*Mr. Paul Egan
(401) 277-6493

Rhode Island Department of
    State Library Services
300 Richmond Street
Providence, RI 02903
Mr. Frank Iacona
(401) 277-2726

Social Science Data Center
Brown University
P.O. Box 1916
Providence, RI 02912
Dr. Alden Speare
(401) 863-2550

United Way of Rhode Island
229 Waterman Street
Providence, RI 02908
Jane Nugent
(401) 521-9000

Office of Health Statistics
Rhode Island Department of
    Health
3 Capitol Hill
Providence, RI 02908
Dr. Jay Buechner
(401) 277-2550

Rhode Island Department of
    Education
22 Hayes Street
Providence, RI 02908
Mr. James P. Karon
(401) 277-3126

Rhode Island Department of
    Economic Development

7 Jackson Walkway
Providence, RI 02903
Mr. Vincent Harrington
(401) 277-2601

South Carolina

Division of Research and
    Statistical Services
South Carolina Budget and
    Control Board
Rembert Dennis Bldg., Room
    425
Columbia, SC 29201
Mr. Bobby Bowers
*Mr. Mike Macfarlane
(803) 734-3780

South Carolina State Library
P.O. Box 11469
Columbia, SC 29211
Ms. Mary Bostick
(803) 734-8666

South Dakota

Business Research Bureau
School of Business
University of South Dakota
414 East Clark
Vermillion, SD 57069
*Ms. DeVee Dykstra
(605) 677-5287

Documents Department
South Dakota State Library
Department of Education and
    Cultural Affairs
800 Governors Drive
Pierre, SD 57501-2294

Ms. Margaret Bezpaletz
(605) 773-3131

Labor Market Information
  Center
South Dakota Department of
  Labor
420 S. Roosevelt, Box 4730
Aberdeen, SD 57402-4730
Ms. Mary Susan Vickers
(605) 622-2314

Center for Health Policy &
  Statistics
South Dakota Department of
  Health
Foss Building, 523 E Capitol
Pierre, SD 57501
Mr. Brian Williams
(605) 773-3693

South Dakota State University
Rural Sociology Department
Scobey Hall 226, Box 504
Brookings, SD 57007
Mr. Jim Satterlee
(605) 688-4132

Tennessee

Tennessee State Planning Office
John Sevier State Office Bldg.
500 Charlotte Ave., Suite 307
Nashville, TN 37243-0001
*Mr. Charles Brown
(615) 741-1676

Center for Business and
  Economic Research
College of Business
  Administration

University of Tennessee
Room 100, Glocker Hall
Knoxville, TN 37996-4170
Ms. Betty Vickers
(615) 974-5441

Texas

State Data Center
Texas Department of Commerce
9th and Congress Streets
(mailing address)
P.O. Box 12728
Capitol Station
Austin, TX 78711
*Ms. Susan Tully
(512) 320-9683

Department of Rural Sociology
Texas A&M University System
Special Services Building
College Station, TX
  77843-2125
Dr. Steve Murdock
(409) 845-5115 or 5332

Texas Natural Resources
  Information System (TNRIS)
P.O. Box 13231
Austin, TX 78711
Mr. Charles Palmer
(512) 463-8399

Texas State Library and
  Archive Commission
P.O. Box 12927
Capitol Station
Austin, TX 78711
Ms. Diana Houston
(512) 463-5455

Utah (BIDC)

Office of Planning & Budget
State Capitol, Room 116
Salt Lake City, UT 84114
Ms. Patricia Bowles
(801) 538-1571
*,**Ms. Julie Johnsson
(801) 538-1036

University of Utah
Bureau of Economic and
    Business Research
401 KDGB
Salt Lake City, UT 84112
Mr. Frank Hachman
(801) 581-3353

Department of Community and
    Economic Development
324 South State Street, Suite
    500
Salt Lake City, UT 84111
Mr. Randy Rogers
(801) 538-8715

Department of Employment
    Security
140 East 300 South
P.O. Box 11249
Salt Lake City, UT 84147-0249
Mr. Ken Jensen
(801) 536-7813

Vermont

Vermont Department of
    Libraries
109 State Street
Montpelier, VT 05609

*Ms. Sybil McShane
(802) 828-3261

Office of Policy Research and
    Coordination
Pavilion Office Building
109 State Street
Montpelier, VT 05609
Ms. Cynthia Clancy
(802) 828-3326

Center for Rural Studies
University of Vermont
207 Morrill Hall
Burlington, VT 05405-0106
Mr. Kevin Wiberg
(802) 656-3021

Vermont Agency of
    Development and
    Community Affairs
Pavilion Office Building
109 State Street
Montpelier, VT 05609
Mr. Jed Guertin
(802) 828-3211

Virginia

Virginia Employment
    Commission
703 East Main Street
Richmond, VA 23219
*Mr. Dan Jones
(804) 786-8308

Center for Public Service
University of Virginia
Dynamics Bldg., 4th Floor
2015 Ivy Road

Charlottesville, VA 22903-1795
Dr. Michael Spar
(804) 924-7451

Virginia State Library
Documents Section
11th Street at Capitol Square
Richmond, VA 23219-3491
Mr. Robert Keeton
(804) 786-2175

Virgin Islands

University of the Virgin Islands
Caribbean Research Institute
Charlotte Amalie
St. Thomas, VI 00802
*Dr. Frank Mills
(809) 776-9200

Virgin Islands Department of
    Economic Development
P.O. Box 6400
Charlotte Amalie
St. Thomas, VI 00801
Mr. Richard Moore
(809) 774-8784

Washington (BIDC)

Forecasting Division
Office of Financial Management
450 Insurance Bldg., Box 43113
Olympia, WA 98504-3113
*,**George Hough
(206) 586-2504

Documents Section
Washington State Library
AJ-11

Olympia, WA 98504
Ms. Ann Bregent
(206) 753-4027

Puget Sound Council of
    Governments
216 1st Avenue South
Seattle, WA 98104
Ms. Elaine Murakami
(206) 464-5355

Social Research Center
Department of Rural Sociology
Washington State University
Pullman, WA 99164-4006
Dr. Annabel Kirschner-Cook
(509) 335-4519

Department of Sociology
Demographic Research
    Laboratory
Western Washington University
Bellingham, WA 98225
Mr. Lucky Tedrow, Director
(206) 676-3167

Applied Social Data Center
Department of Sociology
Central Washington University
Ellensburg, WA 98926
Dr. David Kaufman
(509) 963-1305

West Virginia (BIDC)

Community Development
    Division
Governor's Office of
    Community and Industrial
    Development
Capitol Complex

Building 6, Room 553
Charleston, WV 25305
*Ms. Mary C. Harless
(304) 348-4010

The Center for Economic
  Research
West Virginia University
323 Business and Economic
  Building
Morgantown, WV 26506-6025
Dr. Tom Witt, Director
**Mr. Randy Childs
(304) 293-7832

Reference Library
West Virginia State Library
  Commission
Science and Cultural Center
Capitol Complex
Charleston, WV 25305
Ms. Karen Goff
(304) 348-2045

Office of Health Services
  Research
WVU Health Science Center
P.O. Box 9145
Morgantown, WV 26506-9145
Ms. Stephanie Pratt
(304) 293-2601

Wisconsin (BIDC)

Demographic Services Center
101 E. Wilson St., 6th Floor

P.O. Box 7868
Madison, WI 53707-7868
Ms. Nadene Roenspies
*Mr. Robert Naylor
(608) 266-1927

Applied Population Laboratory
Department of Rural Sociology
University of Wisconsin
1450 Linden Drive, Room 316
Madison, WI 53706
**Mr. Michael Knight
(608) 262-3097

Wyoming

Department of Administration
  and Fiscal Control
Research Statistics Division
Emerson Building 327E
Cheyenne, WY 82002-0060
Mr. Steve Furtney
*Ms. Sharon Lamb
(307) 777-7504

Survey Research Center
University of Wyoming
P.O. Box 3925
Laramie, WY 82071
Mr. G. Fred Doll
(307) 766-2931

Campbell County Library
2101 Four J Road
Gillette, WY 82716
(307) 682-3223

A Process for Identifying a Common Pedagogy and Philosophy

WHAT do we really believe about teaching and learning?

1) Have each participant list five of the most effective practices/activities that they use consistently in their classrooms.

a:_____

b:_____

c:_____

d:_____

e:_____

2) Get them to explain why they use each of these practices.

Practice/activity a:_____

_____

_____

_____

_____

_____

_____

Practice/activity b:_____

_____

_____

_____

_____

_____

Practice/activity c:_____

_____

_____

_____

_____

_____

Practice/activity d:_____

_____

_____

_____

_____

_____

Practice/activity e:_____

_____

_____

_____

_____

_____

_____

3) Help them to use their explanations to infer their own pedagogical and philosophical premises. Just keep asking such questions as, "Why do you really carry out these practices?" and "What do you really believe about teaching and learning that encourages you to carry out these practices?" Help them to make their responses precise, using simple, straightforward words and phrases. Remember, they are trying to define their own beliefs about teaching and learning, not write for you or anyone else.

4) Have the team members share their practices, their reasons for using these practices, and their initial premises with each other. Look for similarities and differences.

5) Identify those practices that are most consistent and get the team to come to a consensus regarding those they can accept. Establish these as the core of the team's pedagogical and philosophical statement.

6) Continue to work on those practices around which there is less consensus, always pushing team members to come to grips with their underlying beliefs about these practices.

7) Make sure that, over a period of time, the team deals with their beliefs on the sections (A – E) included in the tentative philosophy of education proposed in this book, although they may disagree with the specific wording of that particular statement or with entire portions of the statement.

BIBLIOGRAPHY

Aldridge, W. 1989. "Essential Changes in Secondary School Science," cited in *Tech Prep Associate Degree: A Win/Win Experience*, written and compiled by Dan Hull and Dale Parnell, Waco, TX: Center for Occupational Research and Development.

Bailey, T. 1989. *Changes in the Nature and Structure of Work*. New York: Institute on Education and Employment, Teachers College, Columbia University.

Baker, N. C. 1989. "Lamar Alexander on Schools and Business," *Nation's Business*, 77 (April).

Barlow, M. L. 1971. "Changing Goals," in *Vocational Education: Today and Tomorrow*, Somers and Little, eds., Madison, WI: Center for Studies in Vocational and Technical Education.

Barlow, M. L. 1974. "Prologue" in *The Philosophy for Quality Vocational Education Programs*, Melvin L. Barlow, ed., Washington, D.C.: American Vocational Association, pp. 19−22.

Barlow, M. L. 1976. "Implications from the History of Vocational Education," Occasional paper no. 15, Columbus, OH: Center for Vocational Education.

Belcher, C. 1991. "Smoothing the Rough Spots," in *Tech Prep Associate Degree: A Win/Win Experience*, written and compiled by Dan Hull and Dale Parnell, Waco, TX: Center for Occupational Research and Development.

Berliner, D. 1992. "The Failure of Public Education," in *The Failure of Public Education: Fact, Fiction or Fraud?* Columbia, SC: South Carolina Association of School Administrators.

Berryman, S. and T. Bailey. 1992. *The Double Helix of Education and the Economy*. New York: Institute on Education and Employment, Teachers College, Columbia University.

Berryman, S., R. A. Knuth and C. J. Law. 1992. *Preparing Students for Work in the 21st Century*. Oak Brook, IL: North Central Regional Educational Laboratory.

Bonstingl, J. J. 1992. "The Quality Revolution in Education," *Educational Leadership*, 50(3).

Bottoms, G. and A. Presson. 1989. *Improving General and Vocational Education in the High Schools*. Atlanta: Southern Regional Education Board.

Bracey, G. 1989. "Advocates of Basic Skills 'Know What Ain't So,' " *Education Week*, 8(28).

Bruner, J. S. 1973. *The Relevance of Education*. New York: W. W. Norton & Co., Inc.

Butts, R. F. 1955. *A Cultural History of Western Education*. New York: McGraw-Hill.

Caine, R. N. and G. Caine. 1991. *Making Connections*. Alexandria, VA: Association for Supervision and Curriculum Development.

Carraher, T. N. 1986. "From Drawings to Buildings," *International Journal of Behavioral Development*, 9. Cited in Raizen, S. A. 1989. *Reforming Education for Work*. Berkeley, CA: National Center for Research in Vocational Education.

Castell, A. 1964. "Philosophy for School Administrators," a discussion paper presented to the graduate seminar in educational administration, School of Education, University of Oregon, Eugene, Oregon.

Cetron, M. and M. Gayle. 1991. *Educational Renaissance*. New York: St. Martins Press.

Chira, S. 1992. "Are Schools Really as Bad as We Think?" *News and Observer* (April 12). Raleigh, NC: News and Observer Publishing Co.

Chubb, J. E. and T. M. Moe. 1990. *Politics, Markets, and America's Schools*. Washington: The Brookings Institution.

Commager, H. S. 1950. *The American Mind*. New Haven: Yale University Press.

Commission on Attaining Necessary Skills. 1991. *What Work Requires of Students*. Washington: U.S. Department of Labor.

Cremin, L. A. 1961. *The Transformation of the School*. New York: Vintage Books.

Deming, W. E. 1986. *Out of the Crisis*. Cambridge, MA: Massachusetts Institute of Technology Press.

Deming, W. E. In process. *Quality, Productivity, and Competitive Position*.

Dewey, J. 1915. "Splitting up the School System," *The New Republic*, 2 (April 17):10—25.

Donaldson, M. 1978. *Children's Minds*. New York: Norton. Cited in Raizen, S. A. 1989. *Reforming Education for Work*. Berkeley, CA: National Center for Research in Vocational Education.

Ellison, R. L. and D. G. Fox. 1973. *Biographical and Academic Correlates of High School Completion*. Washington: Institute for Behavioral Research in Creativity.

Evans, R. N. 1971. *Foundations of Vocational Education*. Columbus, OH: Charles A. Merrill Company.

Evans, R. N. 1979. "What Is Vocational Education?" An unpublished paper, University of Illinois.

Farnham-Diggory, S. 1990. *Schooling*. Cambridge: Harvard University Press.

Federal Board of Vocational Education. 1918. *The Vocational Summary, Vol. 1*. Washington, D.C.: Government Printing Office, p. 4.

Ferrin, R. T. 1975. *Bridging the Gap*. New York: College Entrance Examination Board.

Finn, C. E. 1989. "Education as Funny Business," *National Review*, Vol. 41 (February 24).

Frankena, W. K. 1966. "A Model for Analyzing a Philosophy of Education," *The High School Journal*, 50 (October).

Gardner, J. W. 1985. *Excellence, Second Edition*. New York: Harper and Row. Cited in *Tech Prep Associate Degree: A Win/Win Experience*, written and compiled by Dan Hull and Dale Parnell, Waco, TX: Center for Occupational Research and Development.

Ginzberg, E. 1977. "The Place of Skill Acquisition in National Manpower Policy," in *The Future of Vocational Education*, Albert J. Pautler, Jr., ed., Columbus, OH: Center for Vocational Education.

Glenn, J. W., and R. A. Walter. 1990. "Vocational Teacher Preparation," in *Vocational Education in the 1990s: Major Issues*, Albert J. Pautler, Jr., ed., Ann Arbor, MI: Prakken Publications, Inc.

Good, C. V. 1959. *Dictionary of Education*. New York: McGraw-Hill.

Gottlieb, D. 1977. "Vocational Education Futures," in *The Future of Vocational Education*, Albert J. Pautler, Jr., ed., Columbus, OH: Center for Vocational Education.

Gray, R. T. 1989. "Education: The Competitor's Key," *Nation's Business*, Vol. 77 (June).

Greenwood, K. 1978. "A Philosophic Rationale for Vocational Education," Ph.D. dissertation, University of Minnesota.

Grubb, N. A. 1991. *Integrating Academic and Vocational Education*. Berkeley, CA: National Center for Research in Vocational Education.

Guzzardi, W. 1976. *Fortune Magazine*, p. 125.

Hammond, J. J. 1977. "What Should Be Taught in the Future?" in *The Future of Vocational Education*, Albert J. Pautler, Jr., ed., Columbus, OH: Center for Vocational Education.

Hodgkinson, H. L. 1985. *All One System*. Washington: Institute for Educational Leadership, Inc./Center for Demographic Policy.

Hodgkinson, H. L. 1989. *The Same Client*. Washington: Institute for Educational Leadership, Inc./Center for Demographic Policy.

Hodgkinson, H. L. 1992. *A Demographic Look at Tomorrow*. Washington, D.C.: Institute for Educational Leadership, Inc./Center for Demographic Policy.

Hook, S. 1967. "What Is Philosophy of Education?" *Saturday Review*, 50 (November 11). Cited in Wingo, M. G. *Philosophies of Education*. Lexington, MA: D.C. Heath and Co.

Hoyt, K. 1991. "Education Reform and Relationships between the Private Sector and Education," *Phi Delta Kappan*, Vol. 72 (February).

Hruska, J. 1974. "Vocational Education: All the Way or Not at All," in *Controversies in Education*, Dwight W. Allen and Jeffrey C. Hecht, eds., Philadelphia: Saunders.

Hull, D. 1991. "Getting off the Ground," in *Tech Prep Associate Degree: A Win/Win Experience*, written and compiled by Dan Hull and Dale Parnell, Waco, TX: Center for Occupational Research and Development.

Hull, D. and D. Parnell. 1991. *Tech Prep Associate Degree: A Win/Win Experience*. Waco, TX: Center for Occupational Research and Development.

James, D. 1991. "Opening the Doors to a Brighter Future in North Carolina," In *Tech Prep Associate Degree: A Win/Win Experience*, written and compiled by Dan Hull and Dale Parnell, Waco, TX: Center for Occupational Research and Development.

Jennings, J. F. 1991. "Congressional Intent," *Vocational Education Journal*, 66(2):18–19.

Johns, T. and J. A. Rice. Personal letter to the author, August 6, 1992.

Jordan, B. 1989. "Cosmopolitan Obstetrics: Some Insights from the Training of Traditional Midwives," *Social Science and Medicine*, 28(9). Cited in Raizen, S. A.

1989. *Reforming Education for Work*. Berkeley, CA: National Center for Research in Vocational Education.

Kademus, J. A. and W. R. Daggett. 1986. *New Directions for Vocational Education at the Secondary Level* (Information Series No. 311). Columbus, OH: The National Center for Research in Vocational Education.

Kaufman, R. and A. Hirumi. 1992. "Ten Steps to 'TQM Plus,' " *Educational Leadership*, 50(3).

Klaurens, M. K. 1975. "The Goals of Education," in *Developing the Nation's Work Force*, Merle E. Strong, ed., Washington, D.C.: American Vocational Association.

Law, C. J. 1975. "A Search for a Philosophy of Vocational Education," An unpublished paper presented to the National Association of State Directors of Vocational Education, May 1975. Available from author.

Law, C. J. 1976. "A Philosophy for Vocational Education," in *Issues and Answers in Vocational Education*. Columbus, OH: National Center for Research in Vocational Education.

Law, C. J. and K. Greenwood. 1977. "Toward Economic Goals and Objectives," in *Vocational Education and the Nation's Economy*. Washington, D.C.: American Vocational Education.

Law, C. J. 1979. "Vocational Education Decision-Making," A paper commissioned by the Bureau of Occupational and Adult Education. Washington, D.C.: U.S. Office of Education, July.

Lazerson, M. and W. N. Grubb. 1974. *American Education and Vocationalism*. New York: Teachers College Press.

Leavitt, F. M. 1914. "How Shall We Study the Industries for the Purposes of Vocational Guidance?" *U.S. Bureau of Education Bulletin No. 14*, Washington, D.C.: Government Printing Office.

Lee, A. 1976. *Learning a Living across the Nation, Volume V.* Flagstaff, AZ: Northern Arizona State University.

Leighbody, G. B. 1972. *Vocational Education in America's Schools*. Chicago: American Technical Society.

Lessinger, L. 1965. "Educational Stability in an Unstable Technical Society," *California Journal of Secondary Education*.

Levitan, S. A. 1977. "An Economist's (Solicited and Surprisingly) Cheerful Message to Vocational Educators," in *The Future of Vocational Education*, Albert J. Pautler, Jr., ed., Columbus, OH: Center for Vocational Education.

Lunsford, J. W. Personal correspondence, 1993.

Lunsford, J. W. 1993. "Total Quality Management (TQM) and Technical Preparation (Tech Prep)," an unpublished paper, which may be obtained from the author.

Miller, M. D. 1976. "A Philosophy for Vocational Education," in *Issues and Answers in Vocational Education*. Columbus, OH: National Center for Research in Vocational Education.

Miller, M. D. 1985. *Principles and a Philosophy for Vocational Education*. Columbus, OH: The National Center for Research in Vocational Education.

Miller, M. D. 1990. "Policy Issue Perspectives," in *Vocational Education in the 1990s*, Albert J. Pautler, Jr., ed., Ann Arbor, MI: Prakken Publications, Inc.

Morris, V. C. 1961. *Philosophy and the American School*. Boston: Houghton-Mifflin Company.

National Center on Education and the Economy (NCEE). 1990. *America's Choice: High Skills or Low Wages*. Rochester, NY: National Center on Education and the Economy,

National Commission on Excellence in Education. 1983. *A Nation at Risk*. Washington, D.C.: U.S. Department of Education.

National Commission on Secondary Vocational Education. 1984. *The Unfinished Agenda*. Columbus, OH: The National Center for Research in Vocational Education.

National Education Goals Panel. 1991. *The National Education Goals Report*. Washington, D.C.: U.S. Government Printing Office.

National Panel on High School and Adolescent Education. 1976. *The Education of Adolescents*. Washington, D.C.: Government Printing Office.

Northeast Regional Exchange (NEREX). 1985. "The National Reports on Education," in *The Great School Debate*, Beatrice and Ronald Gross, eds., New York: Simon and Schuster, Inc.

Organizational Affiliates of the National Tech Prep Network. 1992. "Tech Prep/Associate Degree Concept Paper," Waco, TX: Center for Occupational Research and Development.

Orlich, D. C. 1989. "Education Reforms," *Phi Delta Kappan*, Vol. 70 (March).

Parnell, D. 1985. *The Neglected Majority*. Washington, D.C.: The Community College Press.

Patton, N. 1976. "Seven Cardinal Principles Revisited," *New Dimensions for Educating Youth*. Washington, D.C.: U.S. Office of Education.

Pedrotti, L. and D. Parks. 1991. "A Solid Foundation," in *Tech Prep Associate Degree: A Win/Win Experience*, written and compiled by Dan Hull and Dale Parnell, Waco, TX: Center for Occupational Research and Development.

Perry, N. J. 1989. "How to Help America's Schools," *Fortune*, 120 (Dec. 4).

Prosser, C. A. and T. H. Quigley. 1950. *Vocational Education in a Democracy, Revised Edition*. Chicago: American Technical Society.

Pucel, D. J. 1990. "The Curriculum," in *Vocational Education in the 1990s: Major Issues*, Albert J. Pautler, Jr., ed., Ann Arbor, MI: Prakken Publications, Inc.

Raizen, S. A. 1989. *Reforming Education for Work*. Berkeley, CA: National Center for Research in Vocational Education.

Reel, M. 1979. "Student Organizations . . . Vocational Education in Action," in *Vocational Instruction*, Aleene A. Cross, ed., Washington, D.C.: American Vocational Association.

Resnick, L. B. 1987. "Learning in School and Out," *Educational Researcher*, 16(9).

Santayana, G. 1905. *The Life of Reason*.

Savary, L. M. 1992. *Creating Quality Schools*. Arlington, VA: American Association of School Administrators.

Scanlon, R. C. 1976. "Public Schools for the 80's," Occasional paper no. 20. Columbus, OH: Center for Vocational Education.

Schaefer, C. J. and J. J. Kaufman. 1971. *New Directions for Vocational Education*. Lexington, MA: Heath Lexington Books.

Schaefer, C. J. 1979. "Putting Competency-Based Instruction in Perspective," in *Vocational Instruction*, Aleene A. Cross, ed., Washington, D.C.: American Vocational Association.

Schiller, E. 1989. "Whose School Reform?" *Labor Today*, Vol. 28 (Fall-Winter).

Shoemaker, B. R. 1976. "A Philosophy for Vocational Education," in *Issues and Answers in Vocational Education*. Columbus, OH: National Center for Research in Vocational Education.

Spady, W. 1979. "Competency Based Education: Maximum Confusion, Minimum Implementation," *The School Administrator*, 36(7) (July-August).

Sticht, T. G. 1987. *Functional Context Education*. San Diego, CA: Applied Behavioral and Cognitive Sciences, Inc. Cited in Raizen, S. A. 1989. *Reforming Education for Work*. Berkeley, CA: National Center for Research in Vocational Education.

Stone, N. 1991. "Does Business Have Any Business in Education?" *Harvard Business Review* (March-April).

Swanson, G. Personal correspondence with the author, 1979.

Swanson, J. C. and E. G. Kramer. 1965. "Vocational Education beyond the High School," in *Vocational Education*, Melvin L. Barlow, ed., Chicago: National Society for the Study of Education.

Szabo, J. C. 1991. "Business Support Is Critical," *Nation's Business*, Vol. 79 (October).

Thompson, J. F. 1973. *Foundations of Vocational Education*. Englewood Cliffs, NJ: Prentice-Hall, Inc.

Tucker, W. 1991. "Trustbusters," *Forbes*, Vol. 148 (November 25).

Tucker, W. 1992. "Forces against Change," *Forbes*, 149 (March 2).

U.S. House of Representatives. 101st Congress, 1st Session. *Applied Technology Education Amendments of 1989, Report 101-41*.

Venn, G. 1964. *Man, Education and Work*. Washington, D.C.: American Council on Education.

Venn, G. (circa 1968). "A Message for School Administrators," *Journal of the American Vocational Association*.

Warnat, W. I. 1992. *The New Perkins Act and Tech Prep Education*. Washington, D.C.: U.S. Department of Education, Office of Vocational and Adult Education.

Weatherford, J. W. and J. G. Koeninger. 1974. "Community Interaction: A Partnership for Educational Relevancy," in *The Philosophy of Quality Vocational Education Programs*, Melvin H. Barlow, ed., Washington, D.C.: American Vocational Association.

Webster. 1986. *New World Dictionary*. New York: Simon and Schuster.

Weimer, G. A. 1992. "The Biggest Problem We Have," *Industry Week*, 241 (Jan. 6).

Whitehead, A. N. 1967. *The Aims of Education*. New York: The Free Press.

Wingo, G. M. 1974. *Philosophies of Education*. Lexington, MA: D.C. Heath and Co.

Wirth, A. G. 1972. *Education in the Technological Society*. Scranton, PA: International Textbook Company.

Wirtz, W. 1976. "Community Education Work Councils," Occasional paper no. 17. Columbus, OH: Center for Vocational Education.

Wirtz, W. 1977. "Education for What?" in *The Future of Vocational Education*, Albert J. Pautler, Jr., ed., Columbus, OH: Center for Vocational Education.

Woods, R. A. and A. J. Kennedy. 1922. *The Settlement Horizon*. Cited in Wirth, A. G. 1972. *Education in the Technological Society*. Scranton, PA: International Textbook Company.

INDEX

ABOUT THE AUTHOR

CHARLES J. LAW, JR., was raised on a North Carolina tobacco farm. He has been a vocational agriculture teacher and science teacher at the high school level, a technical college administrator, a university professor, a state director of vocational education (North Carolina, 1969–79), a special consultant to the Bureau of Occupational and Adult Education (BOAE) in the U.S. Department of Education, and the executive director of a regional educational laboratory. He now heads his own consulting firm and specializes in working with local educational leaders as they design, plan, and implement tech prep initiatives.

His degrees include a Bachelor's and Master's in Agricultural Education from North Carolina State University and an Ed.D. in Educational Administration from Duke University. His long-time professional interest has been in identifying and sharing the conceptual base of the most effective practices of vocational education with the rest of the education family. He believes that tech prep offers another opportunity to do that.

Charlie and his wife of 34 years, Camilla, have three children and two grandchildren. They reside in Raleigh, North Carolina.